The King's choir

Singing the Psalms
with Jesus

by Christopher Ash
with Alison Mitchell

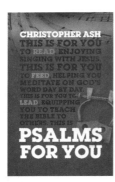

Psalms For You

If you are reading *Psalms For You* alongside this Good Book Guide, here is how the studies in this booklet link to the chapters of *Psalms For You*:

Study One → Ch 1   Study Five → Ch 10
Study Two → Ch 3a   Study Six → Ch 11
Study Three → Ch 3b   Study Seven → Ch 16
Study Four → Ch 5

Find out more about *Psalms For You* at:
www.thegoodbook.com/for-you

The King's choir: Singing the Psalms with Jesus
The Good Book Guide to Psalms
© Christopher Ash/The Good Book Company, 2020
Series Consultants: Tim Chester, Tim Thornborough,
             Anne Woodcock, Carl Laferton

Published by:
The Good Book Company

thegoodbook.com | thegoodbook.co.uk
thegoodbook.com.au | thegoodbook.co.nz | thegoodbook.co.in

ISBN: 9781784984182

Printed in Turkey

CONTENTS

Introduction: Good Book Guides

Every Bible-study group is different—yours may take place in a church building, in a home or in a cafe, on a train, over a leisurely mid-morning coffee or squashed into a 30-minute lunch break. Your group may include new Christians, mature Christians, non-Christians, mums and tots, students, businessmen or teens. That's why we've designed these *Good Book Guides* to be flexible for use in many different situations.

Our aim in each session is to uncover the meaning of a passage, and see how it fits into the "big picture" of the Bible. But that can never be the end. We also need to appropriately apply what we have discovered to our lives. Let's take a look at what is included:

⊕ **Talkabout:** Most groups need to "break the ice" at the beginning of a session, and here's the question that will do that. It's designed to get people talking around a subject that will be covered in the course of the Bible study.

� **Investigate:** The Bible text for each session is broken up into manageable chunks, with questions that aim to help you understand what the passage is about. The **Leader's Guide** contains **guidance for questions**, and sometimes ☒ additional "follow-up" questions.

⊡ **Explore more (optional):** These questions will help you connect what you have learned to other parts of the Bible, so you can begin to fit it all together like a jig-saw; or occasionally look at a part of the passage that's not dealt with in detail in the main study.

→ **Apply:** As you go through a Bible study, you'll keep coming across **apply** sections. These are questions to get the group discussing what the Bible teaching means in practice for you and your church. ⊡ **Getting personal** is an opportunity for you to think, plan and pray about the changes that you personally may need to make as a result of what you have learned.

↑ **Pray:** We want to encourage prayer that is rooted in God's word—in line with his concerns, purposes and promises. So each session ends with an opportunity to review the truths and challenges highlighted by the Bible study, and turn them into prayers of request and thanksgiving.

The **Leader's Guide** and introduction provide historical background information, explanations of the Bible texts for each session, ideas for **optional extra** activities, and guidance on how best to help people uncover the truths of God's word.

Why study Psalms?

I want to invite you to come with me on an introductory tour of the five books of Psalms (the Psalter), to learn to pray. For this is exactly what the Psalms are in the Bible to do—to teach you and me to pray and to praise in perfect harmony with what God wants. The Psalms give a window into how Jesus learned to pray, in his fully human life; and they are how the people of Jesus are to pray as the Spirit of Jesus leads us.

In the Psalms we learn to pray corporately, with the church of Christ in every age. We learn to pray Christocentrically, with our prayers led by Jesus Christ, by whose Spirit we pray them. And we learn to pray empathetically, as we identify with the wider church and focus less on our individualistic (and often introspective) concerns. Learning to sing and pray the Psalms will be a challenging affair, an unsettling experience, and yet a discipline that transforms us into the image of God's Son, the Lord Jesus, whose own prayer life was shaped by these wonderful poems.

The Psalms are God's chosen way to engage our thinking and our feelings in a way that is passionate, thoughtful, true and authentic. They show us how to express our varied feelings; but, more than that, they reorder our disordered affections so that we feel deeper desires for what we ought to desire, more urgent aversion to that from which we need to flee, and a greater longing for the honour of God in the health of Christ's church. The psalms form within us a richer palette of rightly directed emotions. It is not so much that the Psalms resonate with us as that they shape us so that we most deeply resonate with the God-given yearnings they so movingly express.

In many parts of the Christian church today the Psalms are the neglected treasure; many churches are like a poverty-stricken house with incalculable riches forgotten, neglected, moth-eaten and dusty in the attic. So come with me and let us bring the Psalms out and revel in the wonder they offer: a fullness and richness of relationship with God undreamt of by so many of us half-starved Christians.

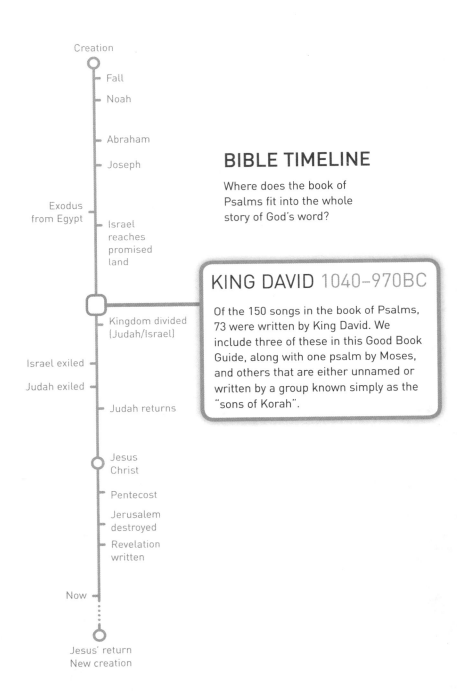

Creation

Fall

Noah

Abraham

Joseph

Exodus
from Egypt

Israel
reaches
promised
land

BIBLE TIMELINE

Where does the book of
Psalms fit into the whole
story of God's word?

KING DAVID 1040–970BC

Of the 150 songs in the book of Psalms,
73 were written by King David. We
include three of these in this Good Book
Guide, along with one psalm by Moses,
and others that are either unnamed or
written by a group known simply as the
"sons of Korah".

Kingdom divided
(Judah/Israel)

Israel exiled

Judah exiled

Judah returns

Jesus
Christ

Pentecost

Jerusalem
destroyed

Revelation
written

Now

Jesus' return
New creation

1 Psalms 1 and 2
BLESSED IS THE ONE...

⊕ talkabout

1. What comes to your mind when you think about the book of Psalms? How do you feel about studying some psalms together?

• Do you have any favourite psalms? If so, which ones and why?

⊕ investigate

Psalms 1 and 2 are like two grand pillars, one on each side of the entrance gate into the five books of Psalms. They introduce Book 1 and head up the whole Psalter.

▶ **Read Psalm 1:1-6**

2. What does the blessed one *not* do (v 1)?

> **DICTIONARY**
>
> **Blessed (v 1):** happy; given good things by God.
> **Chaff (v 4):** husks of wheat.
> **Righteous (v 5):** right with God.
> **LORD (v 6):** the covenant name for God.

• In contrast, what positively defines the blessed person (v 2)?

• And what picture of blessedness are we given in verse 3?

3. Why will those who "stand" in verse 1 "not stand" in verse 5?

• What is the deep reason why both the blessings and warnings in this psalm are true (v 6)?

4. Who is the one person who truly fits the description of Psalm 1 and deserves to inherit this blessing? How do they match this description?

⊡ apply

5. What would it take for you to show more and more the marks of this blessed person?

- What will it look like this week to turn from the pressures of a sinful world and instead delight in the law of God?

⊡ **getting personal**

The life of Jesus, recorded for us in the Gospels, shows us that he was wholeheartedly committed to the belief that blessing is truly found only in a delightful obedience to the law of his Father. Take time to pause and meditate on the wonder of this.

⊥ investigate

▶ **Read Psalm 2:1-12**

6. What are people plotting, and why is it "in vain" (v 1)?

DICTIONARY

Anointed (v 2): chosen by God.
Zion (v 6): Jerusalem.
Decree (v 7): command.

7. What do we learn about "the LORD" in this psalm?

8. What do we learn about God's anointed king in verses 6-9?

• How, therefore, should we respond to him?

⊡ getting personal

The effect upon us, by the Spirit of Christ, of singing Psalm 2 is:

• to subdue our proud desires for autonomy (v 1-3).

• to persuade us more deeply that Jesus really is Lord (v 4-6) and nothing can change that (v 7-9).

• to move us to bow the knee to him now, in this age, before it is too late (v 10-12).

How will you respond personally to each of these three points?

Turn your answers into prayer.

9. Psalm 1 starts with a promise of blessing; Psalm 2 ends with one. How would you sum up in one sentence, from these psalms, how to be blessed?

⊡ explore more

optional

Jesus Christ lived the righteousness of Psalm 1 and inherited the promises of Psalm 2. *In the following verses, how does Jesus match Psalm 2?*

• *Acts 4:25-26 and Revelation 11:18*

• *Matthew 3:17 and 17:5*

• *Hebrews 1:2*

• *Revelation 12:5 and 19:15*

⊟ apply

10. How might you use these two psalms to shape your conversations this week…

- with someone who has rejected Jesus?

- with a Christian who is struggling with sin?

- with a Christian who is facing persecution for their faith?

⬆ pray

Jesus Christ, the righteous One, the King in David's line, is precisely the righteous King that these psalms so beautifully and powerfully portray.

Blessing is poured upon him by the Father. Blessing is to be found in him and in him alone.

Spend some time thanking and praising Jesus, the righteous King.

2 Psalm 22
THE KING'S TRUST

⊕ talkabout

1. When you are going through a hard time, how does that affect your prayer life?

- If you only had one minute to pray before facing a problem, what would you want to say to God?

⬇ investigate

2. Read the words at the top of this psalm (above verse 1). What do we learn from these words?

❯ Read Psalm 22:1-21

DICTIONARY

Forsaken (v 1): abandoned.
Bashan (v 12): a district east of the Jordan river.
Potsherd (v 15): broken piece of pottery.

3. What does David experience in verses 1-2 of this psalm?

• And yet, what does David tell us about God in verses 3-5?

4. In verse 11 David cries out, "Do not be far from me, for trouble is near and there is no one to help". In what way is trouble near in verses 6-8 and 12-18?

• How do verses 19-21 show that David is still trusting in God, even though trouble is so near?

5. Many of the phrases in verses 1-21 are quoted in the New Testament—either spoken directly by Jesus or linked to the crucifixion. Fill in the table opposite to match each quote from Psalm 22 with its New Testament link.

New Testament reference	Linked verse from Psalm 22	Brief summary
Matthew 27:39		
Matthew 27:43		
Matthew 27:46	Verse 1	
John 19:18 (see also 20:25)		
John 19:24		
John 19:28		The king is desperately thirsty

⊟ apply

6. Psalm 22 was written 1,000 years before the death and resurrection of Jesus, and yet David's words so clearly point to Christ. What does that tell you about God's plans to send Jesus as his anointed King?

• How does this help us to trust in the rest of God's plans?

7. In what way is it true for you, or for a Christian you know, that "trouble is near" (v 11)? How do verses 3-5 help you/them to trust in God?

🔆 getting personal

❯ Re-read verses 9-10; then read Psalm 139:13-16

Even for those of us who did not put our trust in Christ until well into adulthood, we were known, chosen and loved by God since before we were even conceived. How does that shape how you see yourself? What impact does it have on how you use your body?

❯ Read Psalm 22:22-31

8. Verses 1-21 could be summed up as "The king suffers intensely; in his suffering, he cries out to God". How would you summarise verses 22-31?

> **DICTIONARY**
>
> **Dominion (v 28):** sovereign rule.
> **Posterity (v 30):** descendants.
> **Righteousness (v 31):** being right with God.

⊙ explore more

optional

❯ Read Genesis 12:1-3 and Psalm 2:8

How does Psalm 22:27-31 echo both God's promises to Abraham and the promise of Psalm 2?

How do we know that this message of rescue will spread to all?

9. Which words or phrases can you find in these verses that show us how to respond to God?

- Do these reflect how you have approached God in the last week? If necessary, how might you change how you respond to God in the coming week to more closely reflect verses 22-31?

⊡ **getting personal**

This psalm takes us on an emotional journey. This is why the people of God have sung it again and again down the ages. Slowly re-read verses 1-21 as you taste the bitterness and the gall of the cross. Now ask the Lord to help you appreciate the wonder of the worldwide experience of rescue and worship that the cross brings about (v 22-31).

⮕ **apply**

10. Verse 31 says, "They will proclaim his righteousness, declaring to a people yet unborn: He has done it!" 3,000 years after this psalm was written, we are some of those "people yet unborn". How could you explain to an interested non-Christian that God "has done it"?

⬆ pray

It is because God proved himself faithful to King Jesus in his affliction that we may be absolutely confident that he will be faithful to us in ours. Thank God for his trustworthiness and pray for those known to you who are suffering right now.

3 Psalm 23
GOD LEADS HIS KING

⊕ talkabout

1. Psalm 23 was written around 3,000 years ago. What do you think were the main tasks of a shepherd at that time?

⊕ investigate

▶ **Read Psalm 23:1-4**

2. What title for God comes at the beginning and end of this psalm?

• **Read 2 Samuel 7:11b-14a.** What covenant promises has "the LORD" made to the king in David's line?

3. What does God do for his king (Psalm 23:1-3)?

• Why does God do this (v 3)?

⊡ **explore more**

In Psalm 23:1-3 there are echoes of the language used in Exodus and Deuteronomy to describe what the covenant God did for the people of Israel at the Exodus and in the wilderness.

Read Deuteronomy 2:7. *How does this link with Psalm 23:1?*

Read Exodus 15:13. Understanding the Hebrew words used here helps us to see the links. "Chesed", the word for covenant love, is used in both Exodus 15:13 and Psalm 23:6, while the word translated as "holy dwelling" in Exodus 15:13 literally means "pasture". *What other links can you see between Psalm 23:1-3 and Exodus 15:13?*

4. Why could David be so confident that the Lord, the covenant God, would lead and guide him?

• And why, when Jesus sang these words himself, could he also be confident that he was following his Father's path? (See John 4:34, 10:17-18 and 12:49-50.)

➔ **apply**

5. What impact does this have on our own confidence, as Christians, that God will lead and guide us?

6. Although the shepherd leads his king to "green pastures" (v 1), where else does the path lead (v 4)?

- Why does King David not need to fear this path? And why, ultimately, did King Jesus not need to fear it either?

⊡ apply

7. Jesus our King has gone before us, into and through the deepest and darkest valley. What difference does that make when we go through trials?

⊡ getting personal

King Jesus has gone through the valley of death for you. How might you most need to rest in this truth this week?

⊡ investigate

▶ **Read Psalm 23:5-6**

8. Verse 5 looks forward to the final victory of the king. What does God do for him?

DICTIONARY

Anoint (v 5): pour oil on someone's head to show they are chosen as king

- How was verse 5 ultimately fulfilled for Jesus, God's King? (See Colossians 2:14-15.)

9. Verse 6 is the climax of this psalm. What final delight does the LORD give to his king?

⤳ apply

10. **Read Psalm 27:4.** This is another of David's psalms. What does he say he most desires?

- What about you? What do you do to "gaze on the beauty of the LORD"?

⊡ getting personal

The King who inherits these covenant assurances is ultimately Jesus Christ. And now they are ours, as we are "in Christ". Our King becomes, with God the Father, our good shepherd, leading us his sheep where he has gone before. Who can you encourage with this thought this week?

⬆ pray

Re-read Psalm 23:6. If Jesus is your King, these words are yours as well. Use them as the basis for praise and thanks.

4 Psalms 42 and 43
TALK TO YOURSELF

⊕ talkabout

1. Do you ever talk to yourself? If so, when and what about?

⊕ investigate

> **Read Psalms 42 and 43**

2. What repeated phrases or sections are in these two psalms?

3. In Psalm 42:1-5, what words show how desperate the author is feeling as he writes?

• In contrast, what does he remember (v 4)?

➔ apply

What the psalmist misses is not some solitary mystical experience of God, but the corporate throng of enthusiastic temple worship, of which he may have been a leader.

4. When Jesus sang these words, what do you think he would have been longing for?

- When we sing these words, what do we long for?

⊡ getting personal

When you meet together with your church family, do you see it as a foretaste of the new creation? How will that help you when you'd rather stay in bed than go to a morning service, or when you find yourself sitting next to someone you find it hard to relate to?

5. In verse 6, the psalmist is still downcast. Where do his memories take him this time?

- In verse 4, he was hearing the joyful praises of the temple crowds. What sound is he hearing now (v 7)?

- According to verses 9-10, what is causing these overwhelming "waters"?

⊟ apply

6. When faced with anguish (v 1-4) and oppression (v 6-10), the psalmist talks to himself. What does he say and how will that help (v 5, 11)?

- It is a moving thought to consider Jesus speaking these words to himself. When may he have had particular need of them?

- When might you need to talk to yourself in this same way?

⊡ investigate

⊳ **Re-read Psalm 43**

7. Psalm 43:1 is the first explicit prayer in the two psalms. What does the psalmist pray for and why?

8. Having reminded himself that God is his "stronghold" (v 2), what does the psalmist ask God to do (v 3-4)?

⊡ apply

Even though the psalmist can look forward to leading God's people in the presence of the Lord, for the moment it's time to sing the troubled refrain a third time (v 5).

9. Knowing wonderful truths about God doesn't remove us from suffering. How does the fact that this pair of psalms returns three times to this same downcast section help when the suffering we experience is long-term or keeps returning?

⊡ explore more

optional

▶ **Read 2 Timothy 3:12; Matthew 5:10-12; James 1:2-4; 2 Corinthians 1:3-4**

What does each one teach us about suffering?

How might you use one or more of these verses to encourage someone who is currently going through trials?

10. The psalmist holds two things in tension: his disturbed state of mind, and his certainty that he will again praise his God. As a result, he can say to himself again and again, "Put your hope in God". Looking ahead to the coming week, when might you need to talk to yourself in this same way?

⬆ pray

During this study we've thought about our own trials and about others we know who are suffering. We've also seen that, however much we suffer, we can still "put [our] hope in God".

Turn some of these thoughts into prayer.

5 Psalm 84
HEADING FOR HOME

⊕ talkabout

1. Have you ever been in a situation where you were longing for home? Where were you and how did you feel?

⊕ investigate

> **Read Psalm 84**

2. Who wrote this psalm?

3. Psalm 84 could be described as a psalm of longing. Who or what is the psalmist longing for?

4. What do we learn in verses 1-4 about God's "dwelling-place"?

    • God's dwelling-place is beautiful. Yet what is the paradox in verse 3?

5. All of these longings find their fulfilment in Jesus Christ. Look up the following verses to see how Jesus fulfils each one: Matthew 12:6; John 1:14; John 1:18; 1 Corinthians 3:16; Ephesians 2:18; Hebrews 9:28. Fill in the table below.

	New Testament reference
Jesus is the One who is "greater than the temple".	
He is the sacrifice offered on the altar for sinners.	
He is the "place" where God tabernacles upon earth.	
He is the one in whom access to God the Father is found by sinners on earth.	
He is the one in whom the life of the living God has appeared.	
By his Spirit, the church of Jesus Christ is the temple of the living God.	

⎋ pray

Look again at the table showing six ways in which Jesus fulfils the longings of Psalm 84:1-4. Turn your response to each one into prayer.

6. There is a blessedness in *being* home (v 1-4), but also a blessedness in *going* home. What do we learn about this pilgrimage journey in verses 5-7?

➔ apply

7. As Christians, we long for our eternal home with the Lord. We walk through life with our hearts set on this beautiful destination. How will this apply in your church family? How can you encourage one another to keep your final home with the Lord in mind as you live your day-to-day lives, in both good times and bad times?

getting personal

The Christian blogger, Tim Challies, writes about a "spiritual first-aid kit" that helps him stay healthy on his pilgrimage (www.challies.com/articles/a-spiritual-first-aid-kit/). What psalms, songs, books, prayers or people help you in your daily walk towards your heavenly home? Is there anything you could add to your own "spiritual first-aid kit"?

⊡ **explore more**

> **Read Psalm 87**

What is the repeated refrain in verses 4 and 6, and the similar phrase in verse 5?

How does Paul unpack a similar idea in Philippians 3:20?

⊌ **investigate**

> **Re-read Psalm 84:8-12**

8. In verses 8-9 the psalmist starts to pray. Who does he pray for and what does he ask?

• In Old Testament history, when this psalm was first sung, who was "the anointed one"?

• Later, as God's people went on singing this psalm during and after the exile, who were they singing about?

9. How are verses 9 and 11 linked?

⊟ apply

10. The promise that "no good thing does he withhold from those whose way of life is blameless" (v 11) has been a precious promise to many suffering believers down the centuries. How can you use this promise this week to encourage a suffering Christian (who is "in Christ" the blameless one)?

⊡ getting personal

What are the signs of God's goodness around you today? Give thanks for each one.

11. "Better is one day in your courts than a thousand elsewhere" (v 10). What is it about your life here that makes this hard to believe? What difference would it make in your life if you genuinely approached each day with this attitude?

↑ pray

- "Blessed are those who dwell in your house; they are ever praising you." (v 4)

- "Blessed are those whose strength is in you, whose hearts are set on pilgrimage." (v 5)

- "Lord Almighty, blessed is the one who trusts in you." (v 12)

Use these verses to pray, first, for your church; second, for individuals in your church family; and, third, for yourselves.

6 Psalm 90
ESTABLISH THE WORK OF OUR HANDS

⊕ talkabout

1. Imagine you're talking to someone who knows nothing about the God of the Bible. Choose a word or short phrase that would help you to describe one aspect of God's character.

⊕ investigate

> **Read Psalm 90**

2. What do verses 1-2 tell us about God?

• Much of this psalm will focus on the fleeting nature—the transience—of our lives. But we begin centred on God (v 1-2). Why is this important?

3. In contrast to God, *our* lives are fragile and transient. What does verse 3 refer to? (See Genesis 2:7 and 3:19.)

• What does Moses say about time in verses 4-6?

→ apply

4. When are you particularly aware that your life is fragile?

• How can you use the truth of verse 4 to encourage a fellow believer who is struggling with how short—or how long—life is?

⊡ getting personal

Think back over the main things you have been praying for recently. Would seeing time from God's point of view change any of those prayers? What else might this view of time prompt you to pray?

5. In verse 12, we pray with Moses "that we may gain a heart of wisdom". That wisdom starts with understanding *why* we are transient and die. What reason do we see in verses 7-11 (see also verse 3)?

6. Life is shadowed by death because we are sinners in a world under sin. But Christians are also "in Christ". What difference does that make? (See Romans 8:1, 10 and 23.)

- As Christians living in a world under sin, what do you think it means to "number our days" (v 12)?

⬇ investigate

> ▶ **Re-read Psalm 90:13-17**

7. In this end section, Moses prays to the "Lᴏʀᴅ", the covenant God. What does he ask God to do?

- How is Jesus Christ the ultimate answer to this prayer?

8. Jesus will have prayed Psalm 90. When might he have needed to apply verse 17 to himself? (See, for example, John 6:66 and 12:37.)

➔ apply

9. If Jesus needed to pray this psalm, we his people most certainly need to pray it for ourselves. But what is the risk for us if we just pray verse 17 but ignore the previous 16 verses?

⊡ explore more

We're not told exactly when Moses wrote this psalm, but we know it was a corporate psalm (mostly written in the plural). One possible context comes in Numbers 21:4-9. *How would Psalm 90 have applied to this situation?*

⊡ getting personal

Psalm 90 puts into our hands a prayer to pray most especially when we are most deeply pained by the fragility of our lives. How will praying this psalm help you this week?

10. Look back to your answers to question 1. Choose one phrase from Psalm 90 that would help you to tell a non-believer a little more about the character of God.

- And choose one phrase that will be an encouragement or challenge to you this week.

⬆ pray

"May the favour of the Lord our God rest on us;
    establish the work of our hands for us—
    yes, establish the work of our hands." (Psalm 90:17)

Thank God for gloriously answering this prayer when Jesus prayed it, by establishing for eternity the work of Christ's hands.

Pray that God will answer this corporate prayer for your church, that the gospel work you do together in his name will bear eternal fruit.

7 Psalm 145
JOIN THE CHOIR

⊕ talkabout

1. In the talkabout for study one (page 7), you discussed how you felt about studying some psalms together and whether you had any favourites. How would you answer those questions now?

⊕ investigate

▸ Read Psalm 145

2. When, and for how long, does David say he will praise God (v 1-2)?

DICTIONARY

Exalt, extol (v 1, 2): glorify, praise.
Dominion (v 13): sovereignty, rule.

- What words does David use in verses 1-2 to describe how he honours God?

• Verses 1-2 pledge to offer God unreserved, unbroken and unending praise. Did David keep this pledge?

3. "If God is not praised, then God is not made known to a needy world." Do you agree with this sentence? Why / why not?

⮕ apply

4. Think of some of the ways that you praise/exalt/extol the Lord in your church family. How can these make God known to those who do not yet know him?

⊡ getting personal

Think of someone you would like to share the gospel with. Pray for an opportunity to praise God in their presence this week.

5. Verses 3 to 13a combine God's greatness and goodness. Fill in the table opposite showing which verses point to each and what they tell us.

Psalm 145	God's greatness	God's goodness
Verse 3		
Verse 4	"Mighty acts"	
Verse 5		
Verse 6		
Verse 7		
Verse 8		"Gracious and compassionate" "Slow to anger and rich in love"
Verse 9		
Verse 10	"Your works praise you, Lord" "Your faithful people extol you"	
Verse 11		
Verse 12		
Verse 13a		

⮕ apply

6. Do you sometimes find it hard to see God in this way—as simultaneously all-powerful and all-good? Why / why not?

😐 getting personal

Do you know someone who is questioning God's goodness right now? (It might be you.) Ask God to open their heart and help them to see the world as he sees it. How can you help to point them back to God's power and goodness?

😐 explore more

optional

❯ **Read Acts 2:22-24 and 4:24-28**

What do these verses tell us about God's involvement in the crucifixion of his Son? .

⬇ investigate

❯ **Re-read Psalm 145:13b-21**

7. Who is God faithful to in verses 13b-16?

• What covenant is God keeping? (See Genesis 9:9-11.)

8. Who is God faithful to in verses 17-20?

• What covenant is God keeping in these verses? (See Genesis 12:1-3.)

• What will be the result for "the wicked" (v 20)?

Psalm 145 was written and sung by King David—but ultimately fulfilled by King Jesus, who could sing it knowing that his praise was indeed *unreserved, unbroken* and *unending* (v 1-2). We are unable to offer perfect praise to God. Ours is *reserved*, it is *broken*, and it *ends*.

9. So how can we praise God in the way Psalm 145 invites us to?

10. As you look back over the seven sessions in this book, what has changed in your understanding or appreciation of the book of Psalms? Which psalm's truths about God have particularly struck you and why?

⊡ getting personal

Look at your answers to question 10. How will you remember those truths about God this week?

↑ pray

"Let every creature praise his holy name for ever and ever" (Psalm 145:21).

This is where we come in—not to initiate the praise, for Jesus has done that, and not to lead the praise, for Jesus is doing that—but to join the choir.

Thank God for sending his Son, Jesus-the-King, who perfectly praises God the Father King.

Ask King Jesus, through his Spirit, to incline your hearts to praise God as you sing in his choir.

The King's choir

LEADER'S GUIDE

Leader's Guide

INTRODUCTION

Leading a Bible study can be a bit like herding cats—everyone has a different idea of what the passage could be about, and a different line of enquiry that they want to pursue. But a good group leader is more than someone who just referees this kind of discussion. You will want to:

- correctly understand and handle the Bible passage. But also…

- encourage and train the people in your group to do this for themselves. Don't fall into the trap of spoon-feeding people by simply passing on the information in the Leader's Guide. Then…

- make sure that no Bible study is finished without everyone knowing how the passage is relevant for them. What changes do you all need to make in the light of the things you have been learning? And finally…

- encourage the group to turn all that has been learned and discussed into prayer.

Your Bible-study group is unique, and you are likely to know better than anyone the capabilities, backgrounds and circumstances of the people you are leading. That's why we've designed these guides with a number of optional features. If they're a quiet bunch, you might want to spend longer on *talkabout*. If your time is limited, you can choose to skip *explore more*, or get people to look at these questions at home. Can't get enough of Bible study? Well, some studies have optional extra homework projects. As leader, you can adapt and select the material to the needs of your particular group.

So what's in the Leader's Guide? The main thing that this Leader's Guide will help you to do is to understand the major teaching points in the passage you are studying, and how to apply them. As well as guidance for the questions, the Leader's Guide for each session contains the following important sections:

THE BIG IDEA

One or two key sentences will give you the main point of the session. This is what you should be aiming to have fixed in people's minds as they leave the Bible study. And it's the point you need to head back toward when the discussion goes off at a tangent.

SUMMARY

An overview of the passage, including plenty of useful historical background information.

OPTIONAL EXTRA

Usually this is an introductory activity that ties in with the main theme of the Bible study, and is designed to "break the ice" at the beginning of a session. Or it may be a "homework project" that people can tackle during the week.

So let's take a look at the various different features of a Good Book Guide:

⊕ talkabout

Each session kicks off with a discussion question, based on the group's opinions or experiences. It's designed to get people talking and thinking in a general way about the main subject of the Bible study.

⬇ investigate

The first thing you and your group need to know is what the Bible passage is about, which is the purpose of these questions. But watch out—people may come up with answers based on their experiences or teaching they have heard in the past, without referring to the passage at all. It's amazing how often we can get through a Bible study without actually looking at the Bible! If you're stuck for an answer, the Leader's Guide contains guidance for questions. These are the answers to direct your group to. This information isn't meant to be read out to people—ideally, you want them to discover these answers from the Bible for themselves. Sometimes there are optional follow-up questions (see ☑ in guidance for questions) to help you help your group get to the answer.

😀 explore more

These questions generally point people to other relevant parts of the Bible. They are useful for helping your group to see how the passage fits into the "big picture" of the whole Bible. These sections are OPTIONAL—only use them if you have time. Remember that it's better to finish in good time having really grasped one big thing from the passage, than to try and cram everything in.

➡ apply

We want to encourage you to spend more time working at application—too often, it is simply tacked on at the end. In the Good Book Guides, apply sections are mixed in with the investigate sections of the study. We hope that people will realise that application is not just an optional extra, but rather, the whole purpose of studying the

Bible. We do Bible study so that our lives can be changed by what we hear from God's word. If you skip the application, the Bible study hasn't achieved its purpose.

These questions draw out practical lessons that we can all learn from the Bible passage. You can review what has been learned so far, and think about practical differences that this should make in our churches and our lives. The group gets the opportunity to talk about what they personally have learned.

😀 getting personal

These can be done at home, but it is well worth allowing a few moments of quiet reflection during the study for each person to think and pray about specific changes they need to make in their own lives. Why not have a time for reporting back at the beginning of the following session, so that everyone can be encouraged and challenged by one another to make application a priority?

⬆ pray

In Acts 4:25-30 the first Christians quoted Psalm 2 as they prayed in response to the persecution of the apostles by the Jewish religious leaders. Today however, it's not as common for Christians to base prayers on the truths of God's word as it once was. As a result, our prayers tend to be weak, superficial and self-centred rather than bold, visionary and God-centred.

The prayer section is based on what has been learned from the Bible passage. How different our prayer times would be if we were genuinely responding to what God has said to us through his word.

1

Psalms 1 and 2

BLESSED IS THE ONE...

THE BIG IDEA

Psalms 1 and 2 set before us a good rule and a good Ruler. Jesus is the Psalm 1 man who is also the Psalm 2 King—the King who is righteous, and the righteous man who is King.

SUMMARY

The first three studies in this Good Book Guide feature four examples from Book 1 of the Psalter (Psalms 1 – 41). Apart from Psalms 1 and 2, almost all these psalms are headed "of David". Together with Book 2, this forms the main "of David" collection of psalms. There is a tremendous focus on God's anointed King—at first David, then David's successors, and finally "great David's greater Son", the Lord Jesus Christ. The word "Anointed One" is "Messiah" in Hebrew and then "Christ" in Greek. David and his successors were, in a manner of speaking, little "messiahs"; they show us something of the character and destiny of the final Messiah, the Lord Jesus Christ.

Psalms 1 and 2 are like two grand pillars, one on each side of the entrance gate into the five books of Psalms. They introduce Book 1 and also head up the whole Psalter. These psalms are bracketed by blessing and conclude with warnings. Psalm 1 begins with a declaration of blessing (1:1, "Blessed is…") and Psalm 2 ends with a blessing (2:12, "Blessed are…"). Each warns, near the end, of a "way" that "leads to destruction" (1:6; 2:12). Together they set the scene and put down critical markers for our whole tour.

Psalm 1 begins with "Blessed is the one who…" (v 1). This is confidently to affirm

that the one to be described is under the favour of God, ultimately happy, the recipient of life, joy, peace and delight. It is to declare that this person will be blessed and that blessing need be sought, and can be found, in no other place. This is an extraordinarily profound declaration. It calls for a decision of the will and heart. Yes, I say, I really believe that this person, and only the person who is described here, will be blessed by God. Even to join in the first few words of this first psalm is a demanding challenge!

Psalm 1 declares a blessing (v 1-3), warns of destruction (v 4-5) and concludes by restating both of these (the blessing, v 6a, and the destruction, v 6b), so that we are in no doubt about the double-edged thrust of the Psalm.

It is often thought that the purpose of Psalm 2 is to celebrate the coronation (or anointing) of a king in David's line. Such a coronation is shadowed by intense conflict, as we shall see. The psalm begins with a shared desire (Psalm 2:1-3); this desire is answered by a twofold declaration (4-9), which issues in a momentous choice (v 10-12).

If there is a calm and measured clarity about Psalm 1, Psalm 2 confronts us with an urgent intensity of contrasting truths.

OPTIONAL EXTRA

Ask each group member what their favourite song is, and why they love singing or listening to it. If you have lots of time, you could find some of the songs online and listen to them, maybe while having coffee or a meal before the study begins. This discussion introduces the idea that songs stick with us and sometimes even shape us. That's why the book of Psalms is here—for us to sing, with Jesus, and be shaped by.

GUIDANCE FOR QUESTIONS

1. What comes to your mind when you think about the book of Psalms? How do you feel about studying some psalms together?
• **Do you have any favourite psalms? If so, which ones and why?**
The aim of this discussion is to introduce the subject of the psalms before exploring Psalms 1 and 2 in detail. Try not to spend too long on this question.

Psalms 1 and 2 are like two grand pillars, one on each side of the entrance gate into the five books of Psalms. They introduce Book 1 and also head up the whole Psalter.

2. What does the blessed one *not* do (v 1)? The blessed one does not walk, stand or sit with those who do not delight in God and his law. To be "the one who does not" do these things—who does not walk with these people or stand with these people—is very hard; for it results in being the object of the mockery of these people. This person may be blessed, but their blessing comes at a cost.

• **In contrast, what positively defines the blessed person (v 2)?** Their "delight is in the law of the LORD". In the deepest depths of their heart they love the LORD (the God of the covenant) and therefore they love his "law". The word "law" (Hebrew Torah) means instruction or teaching. Probably here it refers especially to the whole of the first five books of the Bible (the Pentateuch) and the preaching

of the prophets as they proclaimed this covenant instruction. This person delights in this God-given scriptural instruction. And therefore he "meditates on [God's] law day and night". The word "meditates" in the original Hebrew means more than silent thought; it conveys the idea of vocal and declarative speaking of God's teaching, and also the conviction that what is spoken audibly expresses the innermost convictions of the heart. Here is a person who not only "talks the talk", saying what we might expect a pious person to say, but does so out of the deepest desire and delight of the heart.

• **And what picture of blessedness are we given in verse 3?** The picture is of "a tree planted by streams of water". In a hot climate, the only vegetation that always bears fruit is a tree with roots deep into life-giving water. Here is someone whose roots go deeply into God, the source of life; and so their "fruit" does not fail. In their life you see the fruit of their roots. They "prosper" in every way. They evidence love, joy, patience, kindness, unfailing faithfulness, peace, and so on. And they do so consistently.

3. Why will those who "stand" in verse 1 "not stand" in verse 5? They will "not stand" because there is a judgment coming. Those who "stand" today "in the way that sinners take" now "will not stand in the judgment". They may seem substantial, even weighty and significant; but on that day they will be seen to be insubstantial, blown away like "chaff" at harvest time.

• **What is the deep reason why both the blessings and warnings in this psalm are true (v 6)?** "The LORD", the covenant God, is the reason. He "watches over" (in loving providential wisdom and care) "the way of the righteous". Here is a "way" that goes the opposite direction from "the way that sinners take"; it is a narrow way that leads to life (see Jesus' words in Matthew 7:14), and God watches over those on that way. But there is another way: "the way of the wicked leads to destruction" in the coming judgment.

4. Who is the one person who truly fits the description of Psalm 1 and deserves to inherit this blessing? How do they match this description? The Bible teaches that there is one man, and one man only, who truly fits the description of Psalm 1 and deserves to inherit this blessing. When Jesus of Nazareth sang, "Blessed is the one who…" he believed it with every fibre of his being. He believed it, and he lived it and sought blessing in no other place. Surrounded by pressures to walk in step with the wicked, to stand in the way of sinners, to sit in the seat of mockers, he resolutely set his face against their values, their sneering, their actions. He was mocked most sharply and felt the pain of this mockery with an intensity we can scarcely comprehend. And yet he delighted in his Father's instruction and declared it day and night with unflinching determination. He is the fruitful one. The covenant God, his Father, watched over his way. And therefore he is the man upon whom the blessing of God the Father rests—the one with whom God the Father was, and is, well-pleased (Matthew 3:17; 17:5).

5. APPLY: What would it take for you to show more and more the marks of this blessed person? We need to be careful not to fall into moralism at this point, or to merely see Jesus as an example of how to live like a Psalm 1 person. Instead, it's only when we see Jesus as the blessed man of Psalm 1 that there is hope. For in him, and in him alone, every blessing is to be found. But then, stirred by his Spirit within us, we resolve—under grace and with joy—that we too will evidence more and more the marks of this blessed person. Our resolve to turn from the pressures of a sinful world will be strengthened; our delight in the law of God will be enriched and deepened; our confidence in final blessing and fruitfulness will be emboldened. When deeply troubled by the pressures of a world that insists we conform, the Spirit of Jesus within us will use our praying of this Psalm to stiffen our determination to be different. When struggling with a cold legalism, the Spirit of Jesus will use this psalm to rekindle a delighted love of God's law in our hearts. When anxious and tempted to "two-time" God—professing to be Christian while hedging our bets and still worshipping the world's gods—this psalm will deepen our confidence that the way of Jesus, the Psalm 1 way, is indeed the only good and blessed way to live.

• **What will it look like this week to turn from the pressures of a sinful world and instead delight in the law of God?** Encourage group members to be honest about the pressures they may face this week—at home, or work, or the school gate—to walk, stand or sit in the way of those who don't love God and his law. How can they build in new opportunities to read and reflect on God's word this week? What will help them to return to good habits of Bible-reading and prayer that may have slipped?

6. What are people plotting, and why is it "in vain" (v 1)? The "nations" and "peoples" (v 1), along with the "kings" and "rulers" (v 2), want freedom from God's rule. They rise up "against the LORD and against his anointed". That is, they rebel against the covenant God in heaven ("the LORD") and his rule on earth expressed by "his anointed"—his anointed king, the king in David's line, ruling from Zion. They will not have this king to rule over them. Their plots are "in vain" because they are plotting against "the One enthroned in heaven". There is in heaven a sound of derisive laughter. These people may join the chorus of mockers (Psalm 1:1); but their mockery is answered by a much more terrible mockery in heaven's courts. No one can ever win against God.

7. What do we learn about "the LORD" in this psalm?

- "The LORD" (this title means the covenant God) is "enthroned in heaven" (v 4).
- He has installed his "anointed" king to rule the world (v 2, 6). (Anointing with oil was a sign that someone had been made king, see 1 Samuel 16:12-13.)
- He laughs at those who try to plot against him (v 5).
- He is also angry with those rebels (v 5).
- The Lord "decrees" (v 7) what will happen.
- He gives his anointed one every nation and every person as his inheritance (v 8).
- He warns all rebels to stop plotting and instead serve God and his anointed King, while they still have time to do so (v 10-12)

8. What do we learn about God's anointed king in verses 6-9?

- God's anointed king (v 2) has been installed "on Zion" (v 6). Zion is the city of David (e.g. 2 Samuel 5:7). Many Old Testament scriptures associate Zion with King David and the promises of the Covenant.
- He is God's son (v 7).
- He has been invited by God to "ask" (v 8) for the "nations" as his inheritance, and the "ends of the earth" as his

possession—meaning he will inherit all things.
- He will "break them with a rod of iron" and "dash them to pieces like pottery" (v 9)—meaning he will conquer the world and subdue all the rebellions of verses 1-3. Here is a King who is quite unlike the rebellious kings of verses 1-3, for this King will be the one who exercises the sovereign rule of God on earth, who brings in the kingdom of God. This King is also the Psalm 1 man!

- **How, therefore, should we respond to him?** Our right response is to "kiss [the] son", since he will govern creation on behalf of his father. If we don't, our "way will lead to [our] destruction" (v 12). Here is a sober and urgent warning. Turn right around, repent, from the proud autonomy of verses 1-3. From setting yourself "against" the covenant God and his anointed king, turn around and bow gladly to the rule of God in heaven, expressed in his rule on earth through his anointed king. If you do not do that, if you persist in the verses 1-3 "way", you will be destroyed, just as the wicked at the end of Psalm 1 are on a "way" that "leads to destruction".

9. Psalm 1 starts with a promise of blessing; Psalm 2 ends with one. How would you sum up in one sentence, from these psalms, how to be blessed?

This question will help group members to focus on the heart of these two psalms—which is Jesus Christ. A possible answer might be: "Jesus is the Psalm 1 man who is also the Psalm 2 King, so blessing is to be found in him and him alone."

EXPLORE MORE
Jesus Christ lived the righteousness of Psalm 1 and inherited the promises of

Psalm 2. In the following verses, how does Jesus match Psalm 2?
- **Acts 4:25-26 and Revelation 11:18**
- **Matthew 3:17 and 17:5**
- **Hebrews 1:2**
- **Revelation 12:5 and 19:15**
- The rest of the world plotted against Jesus (Acts 4:25-26 and Revelation 11:18)
- God declared Jesus to be his Son (Matthew 3:17 and 17:5)
- Jesus will inherit the nations (Hebrews 1:2)
- Jesus will rule with an iron sceptre (Revelation 12:5 and 19:15)

10. APPLY: How might you use these two psalms to shape your conversations this week...
- **with someone who has rejected Jesus?**
- **with a Christian who is struggling with sin?**
- **with a Christian who is facing persecution for their faith?**

Encourage group members to think of specific people if they can, even if a need for confidentiality means they don't name them. Psalms 1 and 2 are both short enough to read through with someone as part of your answer.

- You could use Psalm 2 to challenge someone who has rejected Jesus about their need to "Kiss [the] son" while they still can.
- Encourage a Christian who is struggling with sin that Jesus has perfectly lived the righteous life of Psalm 1. Their righteousness is dependent on what Christ has done, not on what they have or haven't done. They can then ask his Spirit to so work in them to help them not give in to the sin they have been struggling with.
- When Christians are persecuted for their faith, they can be strengthened by a reminder that those who tried to rebel against the Lord are, in the end, hopeless in the face of his rule and power. The Lord always wins. See 2 Corinthians 4:7-9.

2 Psalm 22
THE KING'S TRUST

THE BIG IDEA
The king trusts God in the face of desperate suffering.

SUMMARY
This is an extreme psalm. It begins with almost unimaginable depths of suffering, and concludes with an astonishing hymn of worldwide praise.

It may surprise us that God's anointed king expresses such abandonment. After all, is kingship not a position of comfort, wealth, privilege, fame and power? Yet the first part of the psalm is frightening in the intensity of its suffering. The truth is that to be God's anointed king is to inherit a calling to suffer more deeply than we can imagine.

We do not know just what suffering in David's life drew out of him this astonishing psalm, but what we can say is that he is experiencing a foretaste of the sufferings of the Christ. This psalm is quoted or echoed repeatedly in the New Testament (e.g. Matthew 27:39, 43, 46; Mark 15:29, 34; John 19:24; 2 Timothy 4:17,18; Hebrews 2:12). By the Spirit, David voices words that will find their fulfilment centuries later. This means that as we read the psalm, we should be thinking not only of David's suffering, but of Jesus' too.

If you or I were offered the post of king or queen, we would perhaps jump at it. But to be God's anointed King is to inherit a calling to suffer more deeply than we can imagine. In this psalm, King David experiences a foretaste of this suffering. This psalm comes as a terrible shock after the joyful victory that is celebrated in Psalms 20 and 21. There is victory at the end of this psalm too (Psalm 22:22-31); but we reach it only through the sufferings of verses 1-21. There was joy set before God's King; but he attained it only by enduring the cross (Hebrews 12:2).

The Lord Jesus must have sung this psalm many times in its entirety before he cried the first line in agony from the cross. When he cried out, "My God, my God, why have you forsaken me?" it was not because he did not know the answer. He knew—it was the entire purpose of his being made flesh—that he must endure the hell of God-forsakenness to pay the penalty for sinners. And yet, in the agony of separation from the Father whom he had known with loving delight for all eternity, only this psalm can begin fully to express the depth of his suffering. And yet, even as he endured the covenant curse of being forsaken, somehow perhaps the remainder of the psalm spoke to his suffering heart of the joy set before him, and gave him the strength to continue giving himself to the very end, when he could cry, "It is finished!" (John 19:30).

OPTIONAL EXTRA
Handel's Messiah includes a section where Psalm 22:7-8 is set to music. You can find it by doing a web search for "Handel Messiah 'He trusted in God'". Play this section to the group, listening especially for the way the singers repeatedly hurl the mocking phrase "Let him deliver him" around the choir.

GUIDANCE FOR QUESTIONS

1. When you are going through a hard time, how does that affect your prayer life? If you only had one minute to pray before facing a problem, what would you want to say to God? The aim of this discussion is briefly to consider how suffering tends to affect how we pray, before we look at a psalm written by David at a time of immense suffering.

2. Read the words at the top of this psalm (above verse 1). What do we learn from these words? The psalm is headed: "For the director of music. To the tune of 'The Doe of the Morning'. A psalm of David". Like so many psalms, the designation "for the director of music" (and the naming of a tune to use) suggests that it was used corporately by the people of God down the centuries. By the end of it, we shall see why. Unlike Psalms 1 and 2, which we looked at in the previous study, this psalm was written by David. David was the youngest son of Jesse and took care of his father's sheep, and yet he was chosen by God to be the next king of Israel (1 Samuel 16:1-13). David was anointed by the prophet Samuel while he was still a young man. He was then persecuted by King Saul, and eventually became king after the death of Saul (1 Samuel 16:13 – 2 Samuel 2:4). See pages 52-53 of *Psalms For You* for more on David as the author of about half of the book of Psalms.

3. What does David experience in verses 1-2 of this psalm? David experiences agonising distance from God the Father ("so far… so far…") and terrifying silence ("you do not answer"). The covenant God who never, ever "forsakes" his people (for that is the definition of covenant faithfulness) has "forsaken" him. David cannot rest, although

God seems to have no difficulty resting in silent distance.

- **And yet, what does David tell us about God in verses 3-5?** God rules (he is "enthroned") and he is holy (v 3). He is rightly praised by the people of Israel, who were saved by God when they put their trust in him (v 4-5). Notice the threefold "trust… trusted… trusted". We praise you, says the king, precisely because those who put their trust in you are always rescued. You are utterly trustworthy. No one who trusts you is put to shame.

4. In verse 11 David cries out, "Do not be far from me, for trouble is near and there is no one to help". In what way is trouble near in verses 6-8 and 12-18? David is being scorned and despised (v 6), mocked and insulted (v 7). His enemies surround him like bulls, (v 12), lions (v 13) and dogs (v 16). He is suffering physically— "bones … out of joint" (v 14), desperately thirsty (v 15), with pierced hands and feet (v 16). This king is being torn apart and there is no one to help.

- **How do verses 19-21 show that David is still trusting in God, even though trouble is so near?** David calls on the "Lord", the covenant name for God. Despite his suffering, David knows that God has always been faithful to his covenant promises (see also v 3-5) and can be trusted still. So he calls again on the Lord to rescue him.

5. Many of the phrases in verses 1-21 are quoted in the New Testament— either spoken directly by Jesus or linked to the crucifixion. Fill in the table opposite to match each quote from Psalm 22 with its New Testament link. Note: there are more New Testament links in

New Testament reference	Linked verse from Psalm 22	Brief summary
Matthew 27:39	Verse 7	Hurled insults and shaking heads
Matthew 27:43	Verse 8	He trusts in God, so let God rescue him
Matthew 27:46	**Verse 1**	"My God, my God, why have you forsaken me?"
John 19:18 (see also 20:25)	Verse 16	Pierced hands and feet
John 19:24	Verse 18	They divided his clothes and cast lots
John 19:28	Verse 15	**The king is desperately thirsty**

Psalm 22 than the six listed above, though they are sometimes harder to match with specific New Testament verses. For example, when someone was crucified, the physical exertion often caused some of their joints to dislocate (see Psalm 22:14). Also, the Roman soldiers mocked and hit Jesus (John 19:2-3), surrounding him and attacking him like bulls (Psalm 22:12), lions (v 13) or dogs (v 16).

6. APPLY: Psalm 22 was written 1,000 years before the death and resurrection of Jesus, and yet David's words so clearly point to Christ. What does that tell you about God's plans to send Jesus as his anointed King? How does this help us to trust in the rest of God's plans? It was always God's plan to send his Son to be the anointed King (the Christ/Messiah) who would rescue his people. Acts 3:18 and 4:25-28 tell us that this was God's plan from the beginning. It's not merely that God already knew what would happen. Instead, he is the one who planned every moment and whose power ensured everything happened as he intended. Psalm 22 contains many precise details of the crucifixion that can only have been inspired by God. This is just one example of how the whole Bible fits together as God's

perfect word (2 Timothy 3:16). Seeing how God has already kept many of the promises in the Bible strengthens our faith in his sovereign rule. We can always trust him.

7. In what way is it true for you, or for a Christian you know, that "trouble is near" (v 11)? How do verses 3-5 help you/them to trust in God? Encourage group members to share openly, if it is appropriate for them to do so. However, even if some answers need to be kept confidential, every member of the group can answer the second part of the question. Possible answers could include using verses 3-5 as the basis for prayer, looking up examples of how God "delivered" the Israelites when they trusted him (eg: Psalm 136:10-16), or copying out one of God's promises and displaying it where you will see it each day (eg: Psalm 34:17-18).

8. Verses 1-21 could be summed up as "The king suffers intensely; in his suffering, he cries out to God". How would you summarise verses 22-31? Possible answers might include "The king's prayer to be rescued has been wonderfully answered" or "The Lord rescues his anointed king" or even "Praise the Lord, who rescues his people and keeps all his promises".

EXPLORE MORE
Read Genesis 12:1-3 and Psalm 2:8.
How does Psalm 22:27-31 echo both God's promises to Abraham and the promise of Psalm 2?
How do we know that this message of rescue will spread to all?
- God's covenant with Abraham promised that "all people will be blessed" through Abraham's descendants (Genesis 12:3). Psalm 2:8 says that "the nations" will be the king's inheritance. In Psalm 22:27-31 we see these promises being fulfilled.
- According to Psalm 22, the gospel of rescue will spread to "all the ends of the earth … all the families of the nations" (v 27); from those at the top ("the rich of the earth") to those at the bottom of the heap ("those who cannot keep themselves alive") (v 29).

9. Which words or phrases can you find in these verses that show us how to respond to God?
- Praise him (v 22-23, 26)
- Honour him (v 23)
- Revere him (v 23)
- Fear him (v 25)

- Seek the Lord (v 26)
- Remember the Lord (v 27)
- Turn to the Lord (v 27)
- Bow down before him (v 27)
- Kneel before him (v 29)
- Serve him (v 30)

- **Do these reflect how you have approached God in the last week? If necessary, how might you change how you respond to God in the coming week to more closely reflect verses 22-31?** Encourage group members to be specific in their answers to this question.

10. APPLY: Verse 31 says, "They will proclaim his righteousness, declaring to a people yet unborn: He has done it!" 3,000 years after this psalm was written, we are some of those "people yet unborn". How could you explain to an interested non-Christian that God "has done it"? If you have time, divide your group into pairs and ask one member of each pair to explain to the other one what God has done. Then ask the pairs to change role. This may help any who are feeling nervous about answering in front of the group. Then ask a couple of people to share their answer with the whole group.

3 Psalm 23
GOD LEADS HIS KING

THE BIG IDEA
God leads his king—into the place of plenty (v 1-3), through valleys of darkness (v 4), to the place of victory (v 5) and of loving delight (v 6). With Jesus as our King, we share this deep and beautiful assurance.

SUMMARY
The Bible commentator Peter Craigie comments that, "There are few psalms in the Psalter which are so well-loved and well-known as Psalm 23. Its appeal lies partly in the simplicity and beauty of its poetry, strengthened by the serene confidence which it exudes" (Peter Craigie, Word Biblical Commentary, page 208). This is true. And yet one of the problems with Psalm 23 is its anaesthetising familiarity. The words trip off the tongue of anyone who has had any kind of exposure to Christianity in their upbringing or culture. So the words wash over us, giving us a warm religious feeling of comfort, but without (necessarily) much or any understanding. We need to press the intellectual and emotional "reset" button before coming afresh to this beautiful psalm. By the end, I hope we shall delight in it with a greater depth, in Christ.

Although the word is not used, this psalm shares with Psalm 22 the theme of trust. (We looked at Psalm 22 in our previous study.) For the king who trusts God in the face of desperate suffering in Psalm 22 trusts this same God to be his shepherd "through the darkest valley" in Psalm 23. The emotional tone is also different. Psalm 22 is a grand and intense psalm, taking us down to the depths in its first part, and with

trumpets playing exultant joy in the final part. But where Psalm 22 is more like a Verdi piece (in classical music terms), here in Psalm 23 we are perhaps best accompanied by the music of Vaughan Williams. There is a quiet reflectiveness here in the prayer of our King.

The Psalm begins and ends with "the Lord", the covenant God (v 1, 6). So the covenant that God has made with the king in David's line (2 Samuel 7:11b-14) should be uppermost in our minds. This is not a psalm about some generic "god" but about the covenant God of the Bible story, and specifically the God who has made covenant promises to his king (see Psalm 2).

OPTIONAL EXTRA
Either: Ask the group to predict what the top three results would be if you type "shepherd" into a web search engine such as Google. Then type it in to see what you get. Repeat the exercise with "sheep".
Or: Listen to a sung version of Psalm 23, such as "I will trust in God alone" by Stuart Townend or "The Lord is my Shepherd" by John Rutter.

GUIDANCE FOR QUESTIONS
1. Psalm 23 was written around 3,000 years ago. What do you think were the main tasks of a shepherd at that time?
Among other tasks, a shepherd kept the flock together, led them to fresh pasture to eat and clean water to drink, cared for any injuries, and protected the flock from predators. Shepherding is among the oldest occupations, beginning some 5,000 years ago in Asia Minor.

2. What title for God comes at the beginning and end of this psalm?
"The LORD." This title, often printed in small capitals, means the covenant God.

- **Read 2 Samuel 7:11b-14a. What covenant promises has "the LORD" made to the king in David's line?**
  - God will "establish a house" for him, meaning a family line (v 11b).
  - David's descendants will be kings after him (v 12).
  - One of David's descendants will build the temple for God (v 13).
  - One of his descendants will be king for ever (v 13).
  - God will be the king's father, and he shall be God's son (v 14a).

3. What does God do for his king (Psalm 23:1-3)? God leads his king to a place of full provision where he "lacks nothing" (v 1). The words "makes me lie down … leads me … refreshes [me] … guides me" in verses 2-3 all speak of God's initiative in bringing the king to where there is plenty.

- **Why does God do this (v 3)?** The Lord does this "for his name's sake" (v 3). Because God has made a covenant promise to the king—the covenant promise that restates the promises made to Abraham and his descendants—the reputation ("name") of God depends upon his doing what he has promised.

EXPLORE MORE
In Psalm 23:1-3 there are strong echoes of the language used in Exodus and Deuteronomy to describe what the covenant God did for the people of Israel at the Exodus and in the wilderness.
Read Deuteronomy 2:7. How does this link with Psalm 23:1?

The words "I lack nothing" (v 1) echo the experience of Israel travelling through the wilderness, of which Moses told them "you have not lacked anything" (Deuteronomy 2:7). **Read Exodus 15:13. Understanding which Hebrew words are used here helps us to see the links. "Chesed", the word for covenant love, is used in both Exodus 15:13 and Psalm 23:6, while the word translated as "holy dwelling" in Exodus 15:13 literally means "pasture". What other links can you see between Psalm 23:1-3 and Exodus 15:13?**
The words "lead" and "guide" are used in both passages. This is what the covenant God does for his people.

4. Why could David be so confident that the LORD, the covenant God, would lead and guide him? King David's confidence that God would lead him was not wishful thinking; it was a trust in the faithfulness of God to his covenant.

- **And why, when Jesus sang these words himself, could he also be confident that he was following his Father's path? (See John 4:34, 10:17-18 and 12:49-50.)** Jesus knew that he had been sent by God the Father (4:34); that his Father had sent him to die and rise again (10:18); and that every word he spoke was exactly what his Father had told him to say (12:49-50). God the Father had made the path clear to his Son at every point.

5. APPLY: What impact does this have on our own confidence, as Christians, that God will lead and guide us?
We can be confident that God will lead and guide us because what God does for his king, he does for the people of the king. David was the representative head of Israel, so what God did for David, he did (implicitly) for the whole people of God of

whom David was the leader. Jesus is the anointed King, the Messiah, the head of the people of God. So what God does for Jesus, he does for the people of God of whom Jesus is the leader. So, as people of the King, men and women "in Christ", this blessing and comfort is ours too.

6. Although the shepherd leads his king to "green pastures" (v 1), where else does the path lead (v 4)? The path takes the king through the "darkest valley" (NIV) or "the valley of the shadow of death" (ESV). So the pathway to these "green pastures" is the road of suffering, as it was in Psalm 22.

• **Why does King David not need to fear this path? And why, ultimately, did King Jesus not need to fear it either?** David knows that the Lord is with him (v 4). He is still picturing God as a shepherd, now with a rod and staff. The shepherd's "rod" fends off wild predatory beasts; the shepherd's "staff" or crook guides and controls the sheep, to keep them going in the right paths. So David knows that the Lord will continue to protect and guide him, even through the darkest valley.
King Jesus went deep into this valley on the cross, enduring unimaginable suffering. He chose this path, knowing all it would entail—and knowing also that his Father would bring him back to life (Mark 8:31). Even death itself could not stop God the Father from leading his Son into the place of plenty.

7. APPLY: Jesus our King has gone before us, into and through the deepest and darkest valley. What difference does that make when we go through trials? As we follow our King, we too are called to enter the shadow of death, in

small ways through trials and sickness and in deeper ways as we face death itself. Yet even in the darkest trial—in the deepest valley, the place where death itself covers our souls with a darkness so black that there seems no hope—even there we may trust that the Son, who is now our Shepherd, walks with us too, just as the Shepherd Father first walked with Jesus. While we should not take comfort from verse 4 in solitary or individualistic "me and God" spirituality, we may indeed take great comfort from it when we meditate on the security we have in Jesus Christ. Our King has gone before us, into and through the deepest and darkest valley. When we enter that valley, and finally when we enter the darkness of death itself, we do so as members of the people of the King who has gone before. He will take our hands and lead us, as he himself was led by his Father.

8. Verse 5 looks forward to the final victory of the king. What does God do for him?
• There is a "table" laid for a victory banquet.
• There are "enemies", those who persist to the end in opposing God's king. They cannot participate in the banquet; they can only watch in defeated frustration, as their hopes for freedom, so confidently voiced in Psalm 2:1-3, end in failure.
• The king's head is "anointed with oil" in preparation for the banquet, and his "cup overflows" with abundant blessing. At last the king of Psalm 2 will rule the nations!

• **How was verse 5 ultimately fulfilled for Jesus, God's King? (See Colossians 2:14-15.)** On the cross, Jesus triumphed over his enemies. His victory over all "the powers and authorities" was public and final.

9. Verse 6 is the climax of this psalm. What final delight does the LORD give to his king? The goodness and covenant love of God are his to enjoy in intimate fellowship with God his Father for ever. The goal of the drama of Psalm 23 is unbroken delightful fellowship of God the Father and the king.

10. APPLY: Read Psalm 27:4. This is another of David's psalms. What does he say he most desires? To "dwell in the house of the LORD" for ever. To gaze on

God's beauty and seek him in his temple. This is also what David looks forward to in Psalm 23:6.

• **What about you? What do you do to "gaze on the beauty of the LORD"?** Encourage group members to be specific as they answer this question. What do they currently do to gaze on God's beauty? If the answer is nothing, what could they plan to do this week to help them discover and enjoy the beauty and wonder of our Lord?

---

4 Psalms 42 and 43
TALK TO YOURSELF

THE BIG IDEA
Fixing our eyes on Jesus, we can pray Psalms 42 and 43 as we talk to ourselves when troubled and downcast.

SUMMARY
Book Two of the Psalter (Psalms 42 – 72) begins with a group of psalms authored by the "sons of Korah" (42 – 49). Psalms 42/43 and 44, at the start of the book and the start of this group, are both laments. Psalms 42/43 are the laments of an individual, while Psalm 44 is a lament of the whole people.

Although Psalm 42 and Psalm 43 are separate in the original manuscripts, there are good reasons for studying them, and praying them, together. The most obvious is the identical refrain in 42:5, 42:11 and 43:5, beginning "Why, my soul, are you downcast?" and closing each little section, so that we have four verses followed by a refrain, another five verses, another refrain,

and then (at the start of 43) a further four verses and a final refrain. Another link is the words, "Why must I go about mourning, oppressed by the enemy?" in 42:9b, echoed in 43:2b. A third is that all the psalms from 42 to 49 are headed "Of the sons of Korah" except for 43, which suggests it is closely connected with 42 and comes under its heading. Feel free to pray them separately; but in this study I will take them together.

The basic structure is very simple, as we have seen. There are three sections, each consisting of four or five verses followed by a repeated one-verse refrain (Psalm 42:1-5; 42:6-11; 43:1-5). Although the three sections have their distinctives, they also overlap. We have seen that the words "Why must I go about mourning, oppressed by the enemy?" in the second section (42:9b) reappear in the third section (43:2b). Also, the pain of people saying to the psalmist, "Where is your God?" appears in the first section (42:3b) and is repeated almost verbatim in the second section (42:10b). So, although we will look separately at the three sections, it is important not to forget that they are closely interwoven.

Most of us talk to ourselves from time to time. Many of us have said, "I need to give myself a good talking to!" Talking to yourself is not necessarily, in fact, a sign of madness, but is very probably an expression of sanity: asking yourself questions, reasoning with yourself, talking yourself out of one emotional state and into a better frame of mind. It's a good idea. Psalms 42 and 43 show us how to do it! Indeed, they show us how Jesus of Nazareth did it, and there can be no better example than him.

OPTIONAL EXTRA

Ask your group to imagine they are talking to themselves in the following situations. What might they say while walking across a tightrope, about to give a talk to 5,000 people, getting ready for a job interview, following a difficult recipe, gazing at a sunset, painting a picture, about to have a tooth removed?

GUIDANCE FOR QUESTIONS

1. Do you ever talk to yourself? If so, when and what about? This question introduces the idea of talking to yourself and when we tend to do that. In Psalms 42 and 43, the psalmist talks to himself a lot.

2. What repeated phrases or sections are in these two psalms?
- "Why, my soul, are you downcast? Why so disturbed within me? Put your hope in God, for I will yet praise him, my Saviour and my God." This section is repeated three times—in Psalm 42:5; 42:11 and 43:5.

- "Why must I go about mourning, oppressed by the enemy?" (Psalm 42:9 and 43:2).
- "People say to me all day long, 'Where is your God?'" (Psalm 42:3) and "My foes taunt me, saying to me all day long, 'Where is your God?'" (Psalm 42:10).

3. In Psalm 42:1-5, what words show how desperate the author is feeling as he writes?
- "my soul pants" (as the deer pants) (v 1)
- "my soul thirsts" (v 2)
- "tears … day and night" (v 3)
- "I pour out my soul" (v 4)
- "downcast" and "disturbed" (v 5)

- **In contrast, what does he remember (v 4)?** What he remembers is "the house of God"—the temple in Jerusalem—and the people of God gathering for one of the great Old Testament covenant festivals, like Passover ("the festive throng"). He used to "go" there. The word used to describe his "going" may mean that he was a leader, leading the people in that joyful, praising multitude.

4. APPLY: What the psalmist misses is not some solitary mystical experience of God, but the corporate throng of enthusiastic temple worship, of which he may have been a leader. When Jesus sang these words, what do you think he would have been longing for? When Jesus of Nazareth sang this, he was longing not only for the immediate presence of his Father, but for his place as the joyful leader of the assembled people of God.

- **When we sing these words, what do we long for?** When we sing this, we express and deepen an intense longing for the immediate presence of God the Father, for the joy of being in the new heavens and new earth, led by Jesus our worship-leader as we sing songs of exultant praise and joy. This longing is partially satisfied in the joyful corporate worship of the church here on earth.

5. In verse 6, the psalmist is still downcast. Where do his memories take him this time? Either literally or metaphorically, he is in "the land of the Jordan, the heights of Hermon". Mount Hermon was a multi-peaked mountain in the far north of the promised land. The Mount Mizar mentioned in verse 6 may be one of those peaks, although we do not know for sure. The headwaters of the Jordan formed in the Hermon range. Whether or not the writer is literally there, these images speak of a very great distance from the temple in Jerusalem.

- **In verse 4, he was hearing the joyful praises of the temple crowds. What sound is he hearing now (v 7)?** The roar of waterfalls and crashing of waves. The sound of overwhelming waters replaces the joyful sound of thronging crowds. The expression "deep calls to deep" is not reassuring, but frightening. This is Bible poetry for chaos and terror. Not only is he far from the people of God rejoicing in the presence of God; he is under overwhelming pressure.

- **According to verses 9-10, what is causing these overwhelming "waters"?** He is surrounded by enemies. Again, this is not an individualistic psalm. The writer longs for the corporate joy of the people of God; he is surrounded by hostility that inflicts suffering ("my bones suffer mortal agony") and mockery ("my foes taunt me"). And again that haunting question, "Where is your God?"

6. APPLY: When faced with anguish (v 1-4) and oppression (v 6-10), the psalmist talks to himself. What does he say and how will that help (v 5, 11)? He asks the question "Why?" and exhorts himself to continue to "hope in God", confident that the time will come when he will again "praise him" because he is God "my Saviour" (or "my salvation").

- **It is a moving thought to consider Jesus speaking these words to himself. When may he have had particular need of them?** When Jesus was anticipating going to the cross, he was troubled by anxious thoughts and a downcast spirit. See Luke 22:39-44. On the cross, he faced the terrifying flood waters of human hostility and the concrete expression of the Father's wrath pouring over him, drowning his soul in sorrows as they swept over him. And yet in the midst of it all, the Father's love was unchanging (Psalm 42:8a).

- **When might you need to talk to yourself in this same way?** Encourage group members to be specific if they can. All of us face difficult times, when we need to be reminded to put our hope in God. This is especially the case when we face the pressures and troubles that come with following Jesus. **Note:** If any of your group also suffer from clinical depression or anxiety, these verses may seem particularly pertinent. Be careful not to give simplistic answers to their problems. These verses still wonderfully apply because our hope is in the Lord's steadfast love, not in our own feelings. Like the psalmist, we need to tell ourselves the truth about God, and cling onto that even in the midst of deep suffering.

7. Psalm 43:1 is the first explicit prayer in the two psalms. What does the psalmist pray for and why?

- The psalmist asks God to "vindicate" him and "plead" for him. This is the language of the law court.
- He turns to God because he has been falsely accused. Literally he is accused both by "an unfaithful nation" and by an individual who is "deceitful and wicked" (the NIV makes this individual plural). This individual is perhaps the ringleader of the opposition, a kind of Judas Iscariot figure.

8. Having reminded himself that God is his "stronghold" (v 2), what does the psalmist ask God to do (v 3-4)? In verse 3 the psalmist cries for God to send out "your light and your faithful care" (NIV) or "your light and your truth" (ESV). (The word is literally "truthfulness", that is, truthfulness to God's covenant promises.) These are God's messengers or agents to bring light where there is darkness and promise fulfilment where at present there seems to be rejection (v 2). These wonderful embodiments of the love of God will "lead" this believer to Zion, the "holy mountain" where God dwells. When that glad day comes, he will again lead the worship of the people of God at God's "altar" (v 4) and praise with glad songs.

9. APPLY: Even though the psalmist can look forward to leading God's people in the presence of the Lord, for the moment it's time to sing the troubled refrain a third time (v 5). Knowing wonderful truths about God doesn't remove us from suffering. How does the fact that this pair of psalms returns three times to this same downcast section help when the suffering we experience is long-term or keeps

returning? It helps to know that the things we experience in life are mirrored in Scripture. We see that suffering is a normal experience, sometimes returning on multiple occasions. We can see from the psalmist's words that it's fine to come to the lord, again and again, and be honest with him about everything we feel and do.

EXPLORE MORE
Read the following verses: 2 Timothy 3:12; Matthew 5:10-12; James 1:2-4; 2 Corinthians 1:3-4
- **What does each one teach us about suffering?**
- 2 Timothy 3:12—Persecution is a normal part of the Christian life.
- Matthew 5:10-12—It is a blessing to be persecuted because of our faith in Christ. It is a sign that we are members of his kingdom and can look forward with rejoicing to being with him for ever.
- James 1:2-4—We don't just expect trials but can "consider [them] pure joy"! They produce perseverance, which leads to maturity.
- 2 Corinthians 1:3-4—God comforts us when we are suffering, which enables us to also comfort others.
- **How might you use one or more of these verses to encourage someone who is currently going through trials?** If someone is suffering because of their faith, we can use the first two references to reassure them that this is not only to be expected but is also a sign that they are living for Christ. If their suffering is more general, rather than related to their faith, the last two references will encourage them to see how God will use that suffering in their own lives, and as a way of comforting others.

10. The psalmist holds two things in tension: his disturbed state of mind, and his certainty that he will again praise his God. As a result, he can say to himself again and again, "Put your hope in God". Looking ahead to the coming week, when might you need to talk to yourself in this same way? Be ready with your own answer if that's needed to start the conversation.

5 Psalm 84
HEADING FOR HOME

THE BIG IDEA

This psalm is in three parts, each of which contains a reference to blessing (v 1, 5, 12) and each of which stirs in us a facet of longing.

SUMMARY

Book Three of the Psalter has a very different tone to Books One and Two. It smells of exile. The first eleven of the seventeen psalms are from the Asaphite school (Psalm 73 – 83); "Asaph" is probably shorthand for a song-writing society, taking their name from one of the Levites who led the music in David's day (1 Chronicles 15:17, 19; 16:4-6; 2 Chronicles 29:30). The context that dominates the book is Judah-in-exile, in Babylon. Two of the clearest examples are Psalm 79:1 ("The nations have invaded your inheritance; they have defiled your holy temple; they have reduced Jerusalem to rubble") and Psalm 83:4 ("Come, they say, let us destroy them as a nation; so that Israel's name is remembered no more").

In 587 BC the neo-Babylonian emperor Nebuchadnezzar conquered what was left of Judah, razed Jerusalem to the ground, ended the Davidic monarchy, and burned the temple Solomon had built (2 Kings 25; Jeremiah 52; 2 Chronicles 36:15-21). For about 70 years that was how it remained, until under religious teachers like Ezra, prophets like Haggai and Zechariah, and political leaders like Nehemiah, it began to be rebuilt from 520 BC onwards.

Psalms 84 and 87 are songs of Zion, the city founded "on the holy mountain" (87:1; see 2:6). In biblical imagery, this means everything that the old covenant Jerusalem foreshadowed; the place where the assembly of God's people gather under God's anointed King and enjoy access to God through sacrifice. The New Testament clearly shows us that all this is fulfilled in the Lord Jesus Christ and his people; in Hebrews 12:22-24 the writer demonstrates that "Mount Zion" is fulfilled in the assembly of Christ's church. When John Newton, inspired by Psalm 87, wrote his famous hymn "Glorious things of thee are spoken, Zion, city of our God", he rightly understood that Zion today means the church of Jesus Christ, Jew and Gentile, gathered around God's Christ and enjoying access to the Father through his sacrifice.

Psalm 84 speaks to us, not so much of facts (although there are facts) as of affections. To join in the singing of this psalm will cause a warmth and delight to well up in us; it will not only inform our minds but warm our hearts.

We do not know when this member of the "Sons of Korah" wrote Psalm 84. It may have been written before the exile, when the temple of Solomon was standing and pilgrims went up there for the old covenant festivals; perhaps the reference to "autumn rains" (v 6) suggests the Feast of Tabernacles. There seems to be an "anointed one" on the throne (v 9)—a king in David's line. But it continued to be sung during and after the exile, when there was no king in David's line (even if, after the exile, there was a second temple). It is placed now in Book Three, which suggests a special appropriateness at a time of exile. Here is a song for believers of every age who are living as "exiles" (1 Peter 1:1), far from their final home.

It is simplest to take the psalm in three parts, each of which contains a reference to blessing (v 1, 5, 12) and each of which stirs in us a facet of longing.

OPTIONAL EXTRA

(Do this activity before reading the psalm.) Give each group member a piece of paper with the following written on it: "Blessed are those who…". Ask them to write down three possible endings for the sentence; and then share their answers with the rest of the group. The Bible gives many different ways in which God's people are blessed. In Psalm 84 we will see three of them (v 4, 5, 12).

GUIDANCE FOR QUESTIONS

1. Have you ever been in a situation where you were longing for home? Where were you and how did you feel? This question introduces the concept of longing for home, whether that is a geographical place, a person, or a past memory. In our study we'll find that Psalm 84 stirs up feelings of longing, but for a different home.

2. Who wrote this psalm? It is one of the psalms "of the Sons of Korah". This is the same group of song-writers who wrote Psalms 42 and 43, which we looked at in the previous study.

3. Psalm 84 could be described as a psalm of longing. Who or what is the psalmist longing for? Almost every verse refers to "God", "The LORD" or "The LORD Almighty". There are also several references to God's "dwelling-place", "courts" and "house". The psalmist is longing to be with his God.

4. What do we learn in verses 1-4 about God's "dwelling-place"?
- The psalmist loves it (v 1).
- The "dwelling-place" means the tabernacle, and then the temple of the LORD, in Jerusalem. This is the place where the "LORD Almighty" makes his presence known on earth.
- The psalmist yearns to be there (v 2). Both his "heart"—his inner being—and his "flesh"—his bodily existence—"cry out" to be there.
- Sparrows and swallows (small birds) make (or made) their nests there, near to the altar (v 3).
- Those who dwell there are "blessed". These men and women are constantly taken up with glad and heartfelt praise (v 4).
- **God's dwelling-place is beautiful. Yet what is the paradox in verse 3?** The reference to the "altar" reminds us that the beauty of this place is, paradoxically, inseparable from the offering of bloody sacrifices for sins. Only because sacrifices are offered on the altar is it possible for sinful men and women to gain some kind of access to the living God. Because of the altar, this believer can address God as "*my*

King and *my* God" (v 3, my emphasis), the word "my" indicating covenant ties of loyalty. Finally, there will be a perfect sacrifice, offered by the King himself for his people. This great King will be both Priest and sacrifice; in him there is full and final forgiveness and true access to God.

5. All of these longings find their fulfilment in Jesus Christ. Look up the following verses to see how Jesus fulfils each one: Matthew 12:6; John 1:14; John 1:18; 1 Corinthians 3:16; Ephesians 2:18; Hebrews 9:28.
(See the table at the bottom of this page for the answers.)

6. There is a blessedness in *being* home (v 1-4), but also a blessedness in *going* home. What do we learn about this pilgrimage journey in verses 5-7?
- As pilgrims, they find "strength" in God (v 5).
- Their "hearts are set on pilgrimage" (v 5). The word translated "pilgrimage" (NIV) is literally "highways"; in the context this is the highways that lead to Zion, which is why some English translations have "the highways to Zion" (e.g. ESV). The NIV's

"hearts … set on pilgrimage" captures this sense, albeit a little loosely.
- It will not be an easy journey, because they will sometimes find themselves journeying through "the Valley of Baka" (v 6). This is an unknown place in Old Testament history, although the word "Baka" may be linked to the Hebrew word for weeping or sadness. But it is clear from the context that it is a dry and lifeless place.
- The pilgrims "make it a place of springs" and it is covered with "pools" from the "autumn rains" (v 6).
- Such people will "go from strength to strength" on the journey, until, at the end of the pilgrimage, "each appears before God in Zion" (v 7).

7. APPLY: As Christians, we long for our eternal home with the Lord. We walk through life with our hearts set on this beautiful destination. How will this apply in your church family? How can you encourage one another to keep your final home with the Lord in mind as you live your day-to-day lives, in both good times and bad times?
Encourage group members to be very practical in their answers. What can they do

	New Testament reference
Jesus is the One who is "greater than the temple".	Matthew 12:6
He is the sacrifice offered on the altar for sinners.	Hebrews 9:28
He is the "place" where God tabernacles upon earth.	John 1:14
He is the one in whom access to God the Father is found by sinners on earth.	Ephesians 2:18
He is the one in whom the life of the living God has appeared.	John 1:18
By his Spirit, the church of Jesus Christ is the temple of the living God.	1 Corinthians 3:16

or say to encourage others to keep our final destination in mind? And what could others do that would help them?

EXPLORE MORE
Read Psalm 87
What is the repeated refrain in verses 4 and 6, and the similar phrase in verse 5? How does Paul unpack a similar idea in Philippians 3:20?

- "This one was born in Zion" (Psalm 87:4, 6)
- "This one and that one were born in her" (v 5)
- "Our citizenship is in heaven" (Philippians 3:20)

This is the most wonderful news in the world: the offer of a new birth certificate that guarantees that we are citizens of the most desirable place on earth.

8. In verses 8-9 the psalmist starts to pray. Who does he pray for and what does he ask?

- He prays for "the anointed one" (v 9), which is "Messiah" in Hebrew and later "Christ" in Greek. This phrase means "God's chosen king".
- He asks that God will hear/listen to his prayer, and that he will "look with favour" on the anointed one.
- **In Old Testament history, when this psalm was first sung, who was "the anointed one"?** "The anointed one" was a king—every king—in David's line.
- **Later, as God's people went on singing this psalm during and after the exile, who were they singing about?** The last king in David's line was Zedekiah (2 Kings 24:15-20). He was king when Jerusalem was overthrown by Nebuchadnezzar, King of Babylon, and the people were exiled from Judah. But, as God's people went on singing this during and after the exile,

when there was no such king, it became clear that they were singing about a future King—great David's greater Son—Jesus Christ.

9. How are verses 9 and 11 linked? In verse 9 the "anointed one" is described as "our shield" and the psalmist asks God to "look with favour" on him. In verse 11 it is the "Lᴏʀᴅ God" who is a shield, and who "bestows favour". These verses are linked. The Lᴏʀᴅ "bestows *favour*" (v 11) upon us because he answers the prayer for "*favour*" on his anointed King (v 9). All the blessings of God come to the people of the King precisely and only because they are first poured out without limit upon Christ our King. He is the one "whose way of life is blameless" and from whom God withholds "no good thing". He is the one who, in his truly human earthly walk, trusted unflinchingly in the Lᴏʀᴅ Almighty (v 12); he is therefore the preeminent recipient of the Father's blessing, and the one in and through whom all that blessing is poured out upon us, his people.

10. APPLY: The promise that "no good thing does he withhold from those whose way of life is blameless" (v 11) has been a precious promise to many suffering believers down the centuries. How can you use this promise this week to encourage a suffering Christian (who is "in Christ" the blameless one)? It is true for all who are in Christ that nothing God gives to us is anything other than good. This is very hard to believe when we suffer sometimes inexplicable and often very painful hurts. It cannot have been easy for Jesus of Nazareth to believe it. And yet it is true: it was true for him, and it is true for us. God our heavenly Father will never give to us anything except what he knows, in his infinite wisdom and kindness, to be what is truly the best for us. We will often not understand how this can be so; and yet it is. To trust this promise will bring surprising springs of life-giving water to us as we go through the valley of Baka with our hearts set on the day when the dwelling-place of God will, at last, be our dwelling-place too.

11. "Better is one day in your courts than a thousand elsewhere" (v 10). What is it about your life here that makes this hard to believe? What difference would it make in your life if you genuinely approached each day with this attitude? Be ready to start this conversation with an example of your own.

---

6 Psalm 90
ESTABLISH THE WORK OF OUR HANDS

THE BIG IDEA
This psalm begins with our eternal home, takes us down to the depths of our fragility and guilt, and ends with God's grace.

SUMMARY
Book Four of the Psalter has a different feel to Book Three. Most of the psalms here have no superscription (note above a psalm). There is little or nothing about the human king in David's line. The major emphasis is on the security and assurance that comes to the people of God from knowing that the covenant God is the ultimate King, whose sovereign faithfulness guarantees all the promises of the covenant.

Do you long to achieve something worthwhile for Jesus? For your life to count for something? Not to be a complete nobody? We all yearn for that (or we ought to). The big surprise at the end of Psalm 90 is that we are authorised to ask God to "establish the work of our hands"—to make what we do last for eternity.

Although this psalm is often, rightly, used at funerals, it is relevant to any time of weakness and discouragement in our walk with the Lord.

Who sang this song? First, this is a prayer of Moses. It is the only psalm headed "A prayer of Moses". He is called a "man of God", which means a prophet in the Old Testament and then a pastor-teacher in the New Testament. It makes perfect sense for Moses to have needed to pray this psalm. Between his waiting in Midian after fleeing Egypt (Exodus 2:11-22) and his final moments on Mount Pisgah when he could not lead the people into the Promised Land (Deuteronomy 34), Moses knew many times of frustration and disappointment in his service of God. But although this might have been the prayer of Moses alone, most of it is spoken in the plural, as if Moses was leading the people of Israel in prayer at a time of corporate frustration.

As well as being originally a prayer of Moses, who of course lived centuries before the exile from the land he led God's people to the verge of, this psalm comes at the head of Book Four—immediately, that is, after the strong context of Babylonian exile that dominates Book Three. Second, then, this is a prayer at the time of exile—because, both during and after the exile, believers badly needed encouragement that their service of God was not utterly futile, as it must have seemed to be.

Third, this is a prayer of Jesus. Surely the Lord must have meditated on this psalm and prayed that the Father would establish the work of his hands at the many times when his ministry was frustrating and shadowed with failure (for example, in John 6:66; 12:37).

If Jesus needed to pray this psalm, we his people most certainly need to pray it for ourselves. But we cannot pray the final verse until we have prayed the first 16 verses. Psalm 90:1-16 is like the safety filter to enable us to pray verse 17 safely. Without verses 1-16 the prayer that God will make my discipleship a success would become a dangerous and egotistical prayer.

OPTIONAL EXTRA

In today's psalm Moses talks about reaching old age (v 10), so begin with a quick quiz about his age at various points in his life story. Ask people to guess their answers; then look them up in the passages below. How old was Moses when...

• he was put into a basket in the bulrushes? (Exodus 2:2; Acts 7:20 – he was 3 months old.)
• he killed an Egyptian who had been beating an Israelite? (Acts 7:23-24 – he was 40.)
• he saw the burning bush? (Acts 7:30 – he was 80.)
• he and Aaron spoke to Pharaoh? (Exodus

7:7 – he was 80 and Aaron was 83.)
• he died? (Deuteronomy 34:7 – he was 120.)

GUIDANCE FOR QUESTIONS

1. Imagine you're talking to someone who knows nothing about the God of the Bible. Choose a word or short phrase that would help you to describe one aspect of God's character. This psalm uses a number of words and phrases to describe God. We will come back to them at the end of the study.

2. What do verses 1-2 tell us about God?
• God has always been "our dwelling-place" (v 1).
• He created the mountains (huge and seemingly permanent)—in fact he "brought forth the whole world" (v 2).
• He always has been and always will be God, "from everlasting to everlasting" (v 2).

• **Much of this psalm will focus on the fleeting nature—the transience—of our lives. But we begin centred on God (v 1-2). Why is this important?** Whether we are taken off to exile or live in the promised land, our weak and transient existence is rooted in the unchanging home ("dwelling-place") that is God. Before God called creation into being, and before time itself began, God is, and is the home of all who belong to him. He is unchangeably the same, unchanging in his essence, consistent in his providence, unalterable in his affections, not swayed or moved by passions. The security of the remembrance that the eternal God is our home prepares us for the sober realism of what will come next in this psalm.

3. In contrast to God, *our* lives are fragile and transient. What does verse 3 refer to? (See Genesis 2:7 and 3:19.)

Verse 3 refers to us returning to the dust we were first created from. The Creator who formed us from dust (Genesis 2:7) has woven together in the mother's womb an organism of the most wonderful complexity, with astonishing abilities, held together by nerves, sinews, ligaments, neural pathways, and a countless multitude of integrated ties. Dust is disintegrated matter. When the Creator declared, with perfect justice, that we would return to dust (Genesis 3:19), he decreed that human existence will always be shadowed by death. We who in our integration can think, imagine, talk, love, make, desire and delight will one day be taken apart cell by cell, atom by atom, and returned to dust. One day, the Creator will say to you and to me, "Return to dust, you mortal"; and on that day we will die.

- **What does Moses say about time in verses 4-6?** Moses is meditating on the mystery of time. We pass through time like a frail plant in the hot middle-eastern climate, blossoming perhaps with strength and beauty, but then suddenly—all too suddenly—withering. "Time is the medium of our mortality," writes Mays, "and so [is] the favorite focus of our folly … The young think they are immortal, the old despair because their time is over" (Preaching and Teaching the Psalms, James L. Mays). We say that time is on our side; but time is never on our side, for it is shadowed always by death.

4. APPLY: When are you particularly aware that your life is fragile? Answers might include when you have a major illness or hear of someone who does; when you are getting old; when there's a serious car accident near where you live; when you see sporting photos from when you were younger and realise you can't do those things any more…

- **How can you use the truth of verse 4 to encourage a fellow believer who is struggling with how short—or how long—life is?** God doesn't view time the way we do. He is "from everlasting to everlasting" (v 2). And so Moses tells us that God sees "a thousand years" as being as fleeting as a single day or night. All of time—all of eternity—is safely in God's hands. We can always trust him. And when we are rejoicing in the Lord's presence in the new creation, we will see even the greatest crises in our lives as "momentary"—see 2 Corinthians 4:16-18.

5. In verse 12, we pray with Moses "that we may gain a heart of wisdom". That wisdom starts with understanding _why_ we are transient and die. What reason do we see in verses 7-11 (see also verse 3)? The terrible words "Return … you mortals!" (v 3) go back to the judgment of God upon sinners in Genesis 3:19: "for dust you are and to dust you will return". And so, in Psalm 90:7-9, Moses leads us in prayer to acknowledge that the reason we are transient is the righteous "anger", "indignation" and "wrath" of God against our "iniquities" and "secret sins".
We live for "days", but every day is shadowed by the wrath of God. At the end "we finish our years with a moan" (v 9)—a whimper. Even if we live a long life (the "seventy years" that was a very good life expectancy in the ancient world), or a very long life ("eighty"), there is no such thing as a perfect day; each day, even the very happiest and best, contains some shadow of "trouble and sorrow".

6. Life is shadowed by death because we are sinners in a world under sin. But Christians are also "in Christ". What difference does that make? (See

Romans 8:1, 10 and 23.) What was true for Moses when he wrote this psalm is still true after Christ, insofar as our bodily existence is concerned. We have forgiveness in Christ; there is no condemnation for those who are in Christ (Romans 8:1); God is no longer angry with us. But we still wait for the redemption of our bodies, which are "dead" (that is, mortal, dying) because of sin (Romans 8:10, 23). It is not true that Christians do not face death; we do still have to face death, and dying, and sickness, and weakness, and frailty, and ageing—unless the Lord Jesus returns first.

- **As Christians living in a world under sin, what do you think it means to "number our days" (v 12)?** We need to understand from our frailty and our mortality that God's anger against sinners is very hot and great. We need to "number our days"—never to forget that we are forgiven sinners who must wait until resurrection day for the redemption of our bodies. A foolish heart lives as if we were immortal; a heart of wisdom remembers every day that we are transient because of our sin. Then, and only then, will we be humbled under the mighty hand of God.

7. In this end section, Moses prays to the "Lord", the covenant God. What does he ask God to do? Moses is asking God to keep his covenant promises. Specifically, to show compassion (v 13) and love (v 14), that we might be satisfied (v 14) and glad (v 15).

- **How is Jesus Christ the ultimate answer to this prayer?** The ultimate sign of God's compassion and love is the sending of his Son, Jesus. For those who are in Christ, there is joy and gladness now (v 14), and will be for eternity (far more than the "many years … we have seen trouble", v 15).

8. Jesus will have prayed Psalm 90. When might he have needed to apply verse 17 to himself? (See, for example, John 6:66 and 12:37.) In John 6:66, many of Jesus' disciples desert him. In John 12:37, the Jews refuse to believe in Jesus even though they have seen him perform many signs that point to his identity. Surely Jesus must have meditated on this psalm and prayed that the Father would establish the work of his hands at the many times when his ministry was frustrating and shadowed with failure.

9. APPLY: If Jesus needed to pray this psalm, we his people most certainly need to pray it for ourselves. But what is the risk for us if we just pray verse 17 but ignore the previous 16 verses? We cannot pray the final verse until we have prayed the first 16 verses. Psalm 90:1-16 is like the safety filter to enable us to pray verse 17 safely. Without verses 1-16 the prayer that God will make my discipleship a success would become a dangerous and egotistical prayer.

EXPLORE MORE
We're not told exactly when Moses wrote this psalm, but we know it was a corporate psalm (mostly written in the plural). One possible context comes in Numbers 21:4-9. How would Psalm 90 have applied to this situation? Even though God had rescued his people from Egypt, they regularly grumbled against him (eg: Numbers 14:1-4; 20:1-5). In Numbers 21:4-5 they grumbled against the Lord again. As a result, the people are "consumed by [God's] anger and terrified by [his] indignation" (Psalm 90:7) as he sends venomous snakes to kill them. They are faced with the truth that their lives are like that of the grass (v 5-6), they need to

number their days (v 12), and plead with the Lord to relent and show them compassion (v 13).

10. Look back to your answers to question 1. Choose one phrase from Psalm 90 that would help you to tell a non-believer a little more about the character of God. There are plenty in this psalm to choose from. Encourage group members to explain why they think their chosen phrase would be helpful for a non-Christian.

• And choose one phrase that will be an encouragement or challenge to you this week. If group members feel able to do so, ask them to tell the group why they feel the need of this particular encouragement or challenge this week.

7 Psalm 145
JOIN THE CHOIR

THE BIG IDEA
This is the last "of David" psalm in the Psalter—a psalm in which our king leads us in praise.

SUMMARY
The trouble with praise is that when someone exhorts me to praise, I often don't want to.

On the face of it, this psalm does exactly that: it exhorts me to pledge myself to praise—a praise that is unreserved. Further, this is to be unbroken praise, for it happens "every day". And it is unending praise, "for ever and ever". So, if we say verses 1 and 2, we find ourselves pledging to offer God unreserved, unbroken and unending praise. How can you and I do that? We can't.

And yet praise is very important. If God is not praised, then God is not made known to a needy world; for it is by praise that we tell others about God. What is more, if my life is not marked and shaped by praise, I will be in grave spiritual danger of being lured away to the worship of some other god—a worship that promises me a greater joy in life but will deliver nothing, or worse.

So praise matters. There are many ups and downs in the Psalter as the tone shifts from lament to praise and back again to lament. There is no simple unbroken trajectory. But, taking the picture of the Psalter as a whole, there is a gradual movement towards praise. By the time we reach the final five psalms, praise dominates with overflowing exuberance.

So the question is: how are we to learn to praise? This psalm gives us a wonderful answer. The key is to remember that it is a psalm of David—it is, in fact, the final psalm of David in the final arrangement of the Psalter. It is a particularly important psalm of David. The first person to speak verses 1-2—that is, to pledge unreserved, unbroken and unending praise to God—is the king. It was part of Old Testament corporate worship that the king should lead the people in praise as their representative head. That is what David is doing here.

Of course, King David did not succeed in keeping this pledge. There were days—especially the terrible day when he slept with Bathsheba, and the days following that disaster—when his life most certainly did not make God known. And, ultimately, he failed to praise "for ever and ever", because he died!

This wonderful praise that David pledges here, and that the psalms kept calling for, no Israelite succeeded in giving—until, centuries later, a boy sang the psalms in synagogue. And—as he grew up as a child, a youth and a young man—every time he heard the call to praise, there was an answering cry in his believing heart: *Yes! Yes, I will praise. Yes, with every deed I do and every word I speak I will make the Father known* (John 1:18). With complete consistency, with integrity, with perseverance and with perfection, Jesus Christ gave the praise that is pledged at the start of this psalm.

Still today, Jesus the King praises God the Father the King: the King praises the King. Or, to put it more accurately, the divine-human King leads his people in praise of God the Father King.

This is such a relief to us. When we fear that we may be asked to dredge out of our reluctant hearts a praise of which we are not capable, we learn now that we are not being asked to take the microphone to lead the praise: no, we are invited to join the choir of Jesus and to join in the praise he is already leading.

OPTIONAL EXTRA

The hymn "O worship the King, all glorious above" by Robert Grant is partly based on Psalm 145. Find a recording to listen to (there are plenty online)—or sing (or speak) the words together.

GUIDANCE FOR QUESTIONS

1. In the talkabout for study one, you discussed how you felt about studying some psalms together and whether you had any favourites. How would you answer those questions now? This opening discussion gives people the opportunity to say whether their view of Psalms has changed over the course of the Bible studies.

2. When, and for how long, does David say he will praise God (v 1-2)? David says he will praise God "every day" (v 2) and "for ever and ever" (v 1 and 2). This is praise that is unbroken and unending.

- **What words does David use in verses 1-2 to describe how he honours God?** In verses 1-2 there are three words for praise: exalt, praise and extol. They are synonyms—and putting them all together conjures up the picture of a praise that is unreserved.

- **Verses 1-2 pledge to offer God unreserved, unbroken and unending praise. Did David keep this pledge?** King David did not keep this pledge. At times, he failed in extreme ways, such as when he slept with Bathsheba, and then had her husband killed (2 Samuel 11). At such times, his life most certainly did not make God known. And even when David tried to live for God, he still he failed to praise "for ever and ever", because he died! Only one King—King Jesus—could and does give God unreserved, unbroken and unending praise.

3. "If God is not praised, then God is not made known to a needy world." Do you agree with this sentence? Why / why not? It is by praise that we tell others about God. When we tell people how good and great God is, we are praising him. Truly to know God is to praise him. Praise is not the icing on the believer's cake—it is the necessary condition of the true God being known.

4. APPLY: Think of some of the ways that you praise/exalt/extol the Lord in your church family. How can these make God known to those who do not yet know him? Answers can include both formal and informal praise. If someone comes to church with us and hears God praised in words and songs, or if they join a Christian family for a meal and hear him thanked by saying grace beforehand, these "formal" activities will teach truth about God and his character. "Informal" means of praise include such activities as giving God the glory when a neighbour compliments your garden, or explaining why joining your church family on a Sunday is a priority for you.

5. Verses 3 to 13a combine God's greatness and goodness. Fill in the table opposite showing which verses point to each and what they tell us. *(See the table below for the answers.)*

Psalm 145	God's greatness	God's goodness
Verse 3	"Great is the LORD" "Greatness no one can fathom"	
Verse 4	**"Mighty acts"**	
Verse 5	"Glorious splendour of your majesty" "Wonderful works"	
Verse 6	"Awesome works" "Great deeds"	
Verse 7		"Abundant goodness" "Righteousness"
Verse 8		**"Gracious and compassionate"** **"Slow to anger and rich in love"**
Verse 9		"Good to all" "Compassion on all he has made"
Verse 10	**"Your works praise you, LORD"** **"Your faithful people extol you"**	
Verse 11	"The glory of your kingdom" "Your might"	
Verse 12	"Mighty acts" "Glorious splendour of your kingdom"	
Verse 13a	"Everlasting kingdom" "Your dominion endures through all generations"	

6. APPLY: Do you sometimes find it hard to see God in this way—as simultaneously all-powerful and all-good? Why / why not? It is sometimes hard to see God in this way. If he is all-powerful, why would he make a world in which bad things happen? So, if he is all-good, he must not be all-powerful. We therefore either compromise on his goodness, and think he must be a morally mixed-up deity; or we compromise on his power, and assume there are things he cannot control. But David doesn't take that view. David quite unselfconsciously praises God that in his infinite wisdom and power he is both all-powerful and all-good. He praises God for precisely the two attributes that our "problem of evil" says cannot simultaneously be true! No doubt David struggled with this. He didn't hold to these things because he was less sophisticated than us, or not as observant of the world. No, he knew as well as we do that bad things happen to good people, and good things to bad people.

The Bible clearly shows that God is both all-powerful and all-good (see Explore More for some examples). But be aware that you may have group members whose personal circumstances make this hard to accept. Point them back to what they know of the character of God, such as Psalm 145:8-9, but also be ready to listen and respond prayerfully to the issues they struggle with.

EXPLORE MORE
Read Acts 2:22-24 and 4:24-28. What do these verses tell us about God's involvement in the crucifixion of his Son? Jesus was handed over to his enemies by "God's deliberate plan and foreknowledge" (2:23). Those enemies were doing what God's "power and will had decided beforehand should happen" (4:28).

The crucifixion was arguably the single most evil deed ever done by human beings and yet, at the same time, was decreed and willed by God for his wonderful and good purpose to rescue his people. As the poet William Cowper put it, "God moves in a mysterious way, his wonders to perform".

7. Who is God faithful to in verses 13b-16? The people to whom God is faithful are "*all* who fall ... *all* who are bowed down ... the eyes of *all* ... *every* living thing" (my emphases). Here is a faithfulness to all of humankind, and indeed every living being including animals, birds, fish and even blades of grass. There is here an indiscriminate generosity to all without distinction: to the wicked and the righteous, to the complex and the simple, to the rational and the sub-rational, to the sentient and the insentient— to every living thing.

• **What covenant is God keeping? (See Genesis 9:9-11.)** The covenant referred to here is God's promise to Noah, sealed by the rainbow, to maintain the good order of the universe: the days and nights, the seasons, the harvests, and so on. Then, God promised never to let this world become hell on earth. Evil may be terrible, but it will always be restrained in this age. After darkness, the sun will rise. After winter, spring will come. After drought, rains will fall. This is because God, the heavenly Father, "causes his sun to rise on the evil and the good, and sends rain on the righteous and the unrighteous" (Matthew 5:45). Every day of life is a day of God's common grace to all. He made this promise to Noah; he keeps it.

8. Who is God faithful to in verses 17-20? The focus here is on God's nearness "to all who call on him ... in truth" (v 18), "those who fear him" (v 19), "all who love him" (v 20): that is to say, to his people.

- **What covenant is God keeping in these verses? (See Genesis 12:1-3.)** In Psalm 145:17-20 we see another faithfulness, to another covenant; a yet-deeper faithfulness because kept to a greater covenant. The promise that began in Genesis 12 through the covenant with Abraham, was sustained for centuries and was fulfilled in Jesus Christ, is the promise that one day there will be a new heavens and new earth, which will be governed by Jesus Christ, the seed of Abraham, and by all his people in him. And, no matter how kind he has been to everybody, in the end this covenant will triumph. The Lord Jesus made the Father known as the One who is unfailingly faithful to every living being in the whole created order, but above all as the One who demonstrates his unfailing reliability to all who trust him through Jesus.

- **What will be the result for "the wicked" (v 20)?** Those who persist in wicked hostility to this good Creator will finally be destroyed. Until that day, though, every day is a day of gospel invitation and grace.

9. Psalm 145 was written and sung by King David—but ultimately fulfilled by King Jesus, who could sing it knowing that his praise was indeed *unreserved*, *unbroken* and *unending* (v 1-2). We are unable to offer perfect praise to God. Ours is *reserved*, it is *broken*, and it *ends*. So how can we praise God in the way Psalm 145 invites us to? You and I know that simply being exhorted to praise doesn't work. A human being trying to jolly me along and arouse me to praise doesn't get to my heart. But when a man or woman is born again by the Spirit of God, who is the Spirit of Christ, something wells up in their hearts and they find themselves beginning to be willing to join in the great chorus of praise to the Father that Jesus leads, as their King leads them, as a member of his people, in singing the praises of God the Father King. Precisely because the Spirit of our great Praise-Leader indwells our hearts, our joining in comes from the deepest depths of our human personhood. We praise because the Spirit of Jesus really makes us want to join the praise!

10. As you look back over the seven sessions in this book, what has changed in your understanding or appreciation of the book of Psalms? Which psalm's truths about God have particularly struck you and why? Ask group members to write down two or three answers individually before sharing them with the rest of the group.

Good Book Guides
The full range

Galatians: 7 Studies
Timothy Keller
ISBN: 9781908762566

Ephesians: 10 Studies
Thabiti Anyabwile
ISBN: 9781907377099

Ephesians: 8 Studies
Richard Coekin
ISBN: 9781910307694

Philippians: 7 Studies
Steven J. Lawson
ISBN: 9781784981181

Colossians: 6 Studies
Mark Meynell
ISBN: 9781906334246

1 Thessalonians:
7 Studies
Mark Wallace
ISBN: 9781904889533

1&2 Timothy: 7 Studies
Phillip Jensen
ISBN: 9781784980191

Titus: 5 Studies
Tim Chester
ISBN: 9781909919631

Hebrews: 8 Studies
Justin Buzzard
ISBN: 9781906334420

James: 6 Studies
Sam Allberry
ISBN: 9781910307816

1 Peter: 6 Studies
Juan R. Sanchez
ISBN: 9781784980177

1 John: 7 Studies
Nathan Buttery
ISBN: 9781904889953

Revelation: 7 Studies
Tim Chester
ISBN: 9781910307021

TOPICAL

Man of God: 10 Studies
Anthony Bewes & Sam
Allberry
ISBN: 9781904889977

Biblical Womanhood:
10 Studies
Sarah Collins
ISBN: 9781907377532

The Apostles' Creed:
10 Studies
Tim Chester
ISBN: 9781905564415

**Promises Kept: Bible
Overview:** 9 Studies
Carl Laferton
ISBN: 9781908317933

The Reformation Solas
6 Studies
Jason Helopoulos
ISBN: 9781784981501

Contentment: 6 Studies
Anne Woodcock
ISBN: 9781905564668

Women of Faith:
8 Studies
Mary Davis
ISBN: 9781904889526

Meeting Jesus: 8 Studies
Jenna Kavonic
ISBN: 9781905564460

Heaven: 6 Studies
Andy Telfer
ISBN: 9781909919457

Mission: 7 Studies
Alan Purser
ISBN: 9781784983628

Making Work Work:
8 Studies
Marcus Nodder
ISBN: 9781908762894

The Holy Spirit: 8 Studies
Pete & Anne Woodcock
ISBN: 9781905564217

Experiencing God:
6 Studies
Tim Chester
ISBN: 9781906334437

Real Prayer: 7 Studies
Anne Woodcock
ISBN: 9781910307595

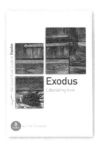

Dive deeper into
the Psalms

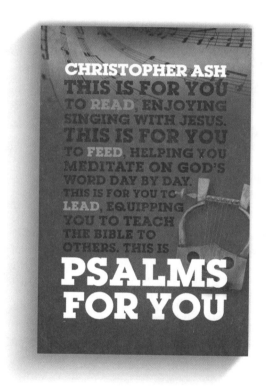

Christopher Ash shows us how to read and apply the book of Psalms. He takes us through 15 pairs of psalms, and helps us to see how they are fulfilled by Jesus and therefore point to Jesus first and foremost, transforming how we read them, enjoy them and sing them. This accessible, absorbing expository guide is for new and mature Christians alike. It has more application than a typical commentary, making it a great resource for personal devotions, as well as useful for leading small-group studies or sermon preparation.

COMPANY

BIBLICAL | RELEVANT | ACCESSIBLE

At The Good Book Company, we are dedicated to helping Christians and local churches grow. We believe that God's growth process always starts with hearing clearly what he has said to us through his timeless word—the Bible.

Ever since we opened our doors in 1991, we have been striving to produce Bible-based resources that bring glory to God. We have grown to become an international provider of user-friendly resources to the Christian community, with believers of all backgrounds and denominations using our books, Bible studies, devotionals, evangelistic resources, and DVD-based courses.

We want to equip ordinary Christians to live for Christ day by day, and churches to grow in their knowledge of God, their love for one another, and the effectiveness of their outreach.

Call us for a discussion of your needs or visit one of our local websites for more information on the resources and services we provide.

Your friends at The Good Book Company

thegoodbook.com | thegoodbook.co.uk
thegoodbook.com.au | thegoodbook.co.nz
thegoodbook.co.in